The Y2K Tidal Wave

Year 2000 Economic Survival

Donald S. McAlvany

Frontier Research Publications, Inc.
P.O. Box 129, Station "U", Toronto, Ontario м8z 5м4

The Y2K Tidal Wave

Copyright 1999 by Donald S. McAlvany

Library of Congress Cataloguing in Publishing Data:

McAlvany, Donald S.
The Y2K Tidal Wave: Year 2000 Economic Survival

1. Eschatology   2. Year 2000 Computer Crisis
3. Finance – Investments
1. Title

January 1999   Frontier Research Publications, Inc.

ISBN 0-921714-54-8

Unless otherwise indicated, Scriptural quotations are from the New International Version.

Cover design: The Riordon Design Group
Printed in Canada: Harmony Printing Limited

Table of Contents

Foreword
by Grant R. Jeffrey

I am very pleased to introduce *The Y2K Tidal Wave* to you as the best documented source I have seen that deals extensively with the economic and financial impact of the approaching Y2K computer crises that will impact every one of us. Over the last ten years, I have come to know and respect my friend Don McAlvany as a brilliant economic analyst and a trustworthy researcher. In addition, Don is a committed Christian who possesses a profound understanding of the critical issues facing our nation as we enter the new millennium. The years ahead will be the most exciting, dangerous, and challenging that we have known in our generation. However, the information in this excellent book will enable you to develop a mature and balanced understanding of the reasons for this crisis, the extent of the danger, and the strategies you need to implement to protect your family from the worst disruptions that inevitably lie ahead. Don demonstrates that Y2K is a crisis that can be survived with a minimum of disruption if we will prayerfully and knowledgeably prepare in the time that remains before millions of faulty computers begin to fail on January 1, 2000.

Donald S. McAlvany is the highly-respected editor of the *McAlvany Intelligence Advisor* that I have used as a valued research source for more than ten years. In the last decade I have found his articles to be well-researched, accurate, and highly insightful of developing trends that will profoundly affect the lives of all concerned citizens. His monthly intelligence newsletter provides penetrating analysis of developing global, economic, political, and financial trends and their affect on our families and personal finances. With an extensive background in intelligence work, McAlvany is often sought out by high-level political and business leaders throughout the world for consultation on global financial trends. He is a well-respected speaker on radio programs and at Christian, political, monetary, and investment conferences worldwide.

The Y2K Tidal Wave documents how the global chaos and confusion during the approaching Y2K computer crisis in 2000 may set the stage for the rise of the Antichrist, the cashless society, and the ultimate return of Christ. In my book, *The Millennium Meltdown*, I primarily focussed on the spiritual and prophetic implications of the Y2K crisis. Don provides his unique perspective on this crisis by focussing on the financial and economic implications of the breakdown of our computer systems and the steps we must take to avoid losing our business and life-savings in the inevitable disruptions to the international financial system that lie just ahead.

McAlvany explores how the dangerous combination of the Y2K crisis, weakened stock markets, and the failure of national leadership may lead to the collapse of our fragile global financial system. This computer technology crisis is unique in human history because it is the first disaster where we know in advance precisely when it will occur. However, McAlvany demonstrates that we have run out of time to fully fix all of the vulnerable computer systems, millions of PCs, and billions of embedded microchips that run our modern world. He examines the extent of the Y2K crisis and how it endangers our utilities, food supplies, and the global financial system. Perhaps most importantly, Don uses his extensive research background to develop practical strategies to protect your family, your life-savings, and small business during this extraordinary crisis.

I highly recommend *The Y2K Tidal Wave* to anyone who wishess to understand the true story behind the headlines and superficial coverage in our newspapers and on television. Don McAlvany will take you behind the scenes to show you the key issues and dangers, plus the practical and financial strategies that will allow your family to survive and prosper as we enter the new millennium trusting in the wisdom provided by our Lord Jesus Christ.

Ultimatly, both Don and I strongly recommend the advice found in the Book of Proverbs:

> Trust in the Lord with all thine heart; and lean not unto thine own understanding. In all thy ways acknowledge him, and he shall direct thy paths.
>
> Proverbs 3:6

Grant R. Jeffrey
Author of *The Millennium Meltdown*
January 1, 1999

Introduction

For the past few decades, the world has been fascinated with the year 2000 — the new millennium. For many students of Bible prophecy, the new millennium represents the onset of the time of the Antichrist, the Great Tribulation, Armageddon, and the Second Coming of Jesus Christ.

For New Agers, the year 2000 represents the dawning of the Age of Aquarius. For the occultists and Satan worshipers, it heralds the entrance of a great world leader. For many futurists, the year 2000 represents a time of great global catastrophe and upheaval. Globalist groups, from the Bilderbergers to the Club of Rome, from the Council on Foreign Relations and Trilateral Commission to the Socialist International, look to the millennium as the era when a new world government (the New World Order or New Civilization) will be launched.

However, for thousands of computer programmers around the world, the year 2000 represents the meltdown of our high-tech computerized world. January 1, 2000 may be the beginning of a cyber nightmare that could crash the global financial system and throw governments, economies, transportation, power generators, and our entire high-tech civilization into total chaos and gridlock. Of all possible year 2000/millennial scenarios, the one that is guaranteed to occur, beginning at midnight on December 31, 1999, is the coming computer crisis.

Our society has practically has made a god out of technology. But we could see that god come tumbling down like the Tower of Babel — all because of a date-related computer bug that inadvertently was programmed into the world's computer system over the past 30 years. Our sophisticated world (now almost completely dependent on computers), which has long since forgotten how to do virtually anything manually, could see that high-tech edifice collapse at the beginning of the new millennium. Perhaps the New Age, the "dawning of the Age of Aquarius," will herald our worst nightmare — a period of the greatest global turmoil and chaos known in history.

The Y2K crisis is looming larger and larger with every day that passes. The more the experts learn about it, the more terrified they become. Every area of our lives will be affected: government, business, telecommunications, the power grid, air transportation, rail/truck deliveries, food distribution, the financial system, manufacturing, and medical care.

There are a number of responses to the coming computer crisis: 1) ignorance — "I never heard of it"; 2) denial — "It can't happen"; "it's nonsense"; "it's only two digits"; "a friend who works with computers says it's no big deal"; "if there is a problem, there's a simple, silver-bullet solution that will be announced shortly"; 3) awareness and concern — "this thing is huge, getting bigger, and needs massive corrective action"; and 4) panic — "the end of Western civilization is approaching"; "we can see a return to the horse-and-buggy days of the 1800s."

Most Americans fall into the first two categories (i.e., ignorance and denial), but a growing number of people are beginning to awaken to the danger and some are beginning to panic. Even the mainline media are finally beginning to focus on the millennium bug.

The Y2K crisis is huge. It could (indeed, is likely to) precipitate a global financial collapse and cause severe economic, financial, and social dislocations for a number of weeks or months. In conjunction with the Asian/global financial meltdown, the Y2K crisis could burst the biggest financial bubble in world history. It is possible, also, that a power-hungry Clinton administration could use the crisis to try to usurp a tremendous amount of financial and political power, much as Franklin Roosevelt did in 1933 in the midst of the Great Depression.

It is ironic that the millennium bug is scheduled to arrive in the same year (the year 2000) that prophets, soothsayers, New Agers, occultists, globalists (the New World Order crowd), and students of Bible prophecy have long believed would herald a time of great change, up-heaval, convulsion, and new beginnings —a major, global paradigm shift. The entrance into the new millennium will not be dull; in fact, it could be catastrophic.

It is also ironic that the millennium bug has emerged at a time when the world's financial system is more fragile than at any time in 70 years (since 1929) or, more accurately, in several hundred years.

For the past several years, I have been forecasting (along with a few other lonely voices crying in the wilderness) a very unpopular message — a time of great financial, social, and political upheaval is approaching that will shake the foundations of America and the entire world.

I have written frequently about the giant global speculative bubble — (especially in America); about the very shaky $125 trillion global-debt pyramid (with over $40 trillion in debt in the United States, including financial derivatives); about the socialistic tendencies and corruption in our government; about efforts of the global socialists to set up a world government; about a coming persecution of Christians and traditionalists who oppose this world government; and about the destruction of America's Constitution.

My analysis suggested that there will be an event (or series of events) — probably unexpected — that will trigger this great collapse. I believe that such a trigger could include one or more of the following: the collapse of the U.S. dollar; a sudden massive dumping of U.S. Treasury paper by foreigners; a new Middle East war; new scandals that could take down a very corrupt, socialist president and his administration; an unexpected collapse and meltdown of the high-flying Asian financial system; a collapse of the vastly overpriced U.S. stock market; and a dozen other possible triggers.

It appears now, however, that the biggest problem of all could be the millennium bug — an unprecedented crisis that will touch and negatively impact virtually every aspect of western civilization.

I have watched the millennium bug phenomenon from a distance for several years and, frankly, was a bit of a skeptic about its potential severity — until the past year. It had seemed to me that it just couldn't be as bad or as apocalyptic as the pessimists were warning.

Over the past year, however, I have talked to dozens of computer experts and voraciously read everything available about the Y2K problem. Interestingly, the greatest plethora of information on the subject is found on the Internet. A few good books and maverick newsletters (such as Gary North's *Remnant Review*) also have emerged over the past year or so that have analyzed the problem in depth. The mainline media, however, have ignored the story, with the exception of recent articles in *Newsweek, The Economist, Business Week,* and several national and foreign newspapers. However, currently an explosion of serious articles has begun to appear.

The more one reads and talks with computer people who are actually in the trenches trying to fix the problem (as opposed to businesspeople, bankers, and stockbrokers, politicians, and government bureaucrats, who wish to remain perpetual optimists), the more concerned and pessimistic one becomes.

The greatest concern is that we could experience a giant global "rogue wave" coming together. A "rogue wave" in the ocean is a fluke combination of several waves whose amplitudes and periods happen to merge by random chance. All their energies combine into one killer wave, which, under ordinary circumstances, would never occur. It is possible that a consequence of global economic events could become one colossal economic/financial "rogue wave" that hits western civilization as we approach the year 2000. If that occurs, will you be ready?

The Y2K Tidal Wave

Part I

Governments acted too late when a single assassination started World War I, and again too late when Hitler began World War II. Their main faults were complacency and disbelief in the danger. Now our lives and well-being are in danger from our own lack of foresight, for we have allowed the computer to usurp our thought and action processes. We cannot return to our old ways — we've forgotten how, and it's too late.

> — R. W. Bemer, computer programming pioneer, and the "father of ASCII code"

The Y2K virus has infected all the vital organs of our global body. A failure in one system could corrupt other systems. Software system repairs are not as rigorous as most people believe. There is no silver bullet.

> — Ed Yardeni, chief economic forecaster of Deutche Morgan Grenfeld bank

The Two Thousand [Y2K] problem lies at the heart of our economy. Today our economy runs on the energy of information. To cripple the technological flow throughout the world is to bring it to a virtual standstill. To delay our efforts is to be inexcusably reckless.

— Bill Bennett, U.S. Senator

Failure to achieve compliance with the year 2000 will jeopardize our way of life on this planet for some time to come.

— Arthur Gross, former chief information officer for the IRS

The year 2000 problem is unique in human history. There has never been a man-made technical problem that will impact so many businesses, so many government groups, and cause so many problems at a personal level . . . The year 2000 problem is unique in that it has at least the potential to affect more computer systems at the same time than any other known event except the electromagnetic pulse from a nuclear explosion.

— Capers Jones, *The Year 2000 Software Problem*

1

What Is the Millennium Bug?

The terms "millennium bug" and "Y2K" refer to how a computer's internal clock will interpret the date in the year 2000. About 30 years ago, computer programmers, faced with a problem of limited and expensive space in the memory banks of mainframe computers, made an innocent but catastrophic decision about how dates would be recorded in computer programs and hardware. In order to save memory, the programmers decided to record the year in the "date field" with only two digits (98) instead of four digits (1998).

While today's computers use relatively cheap silicon memory chips that contain large amounts of memory, the memory systems of the old mainframe computers were constructed of stiff cardboard. These cardboard cards, called Hollerith cards, contained only 80 spaces for memory. Hence the decision to use two-digit dates. Computer programs were instructed to always assume that

"19" should be placed in front of a two-digit year date, such as "98." That standard practice of abbreviating dates continued over the next three decades, until the last few years.

The problem with this method is that "oo," as in the year 2000, will be read by most mainframe computers as 1900 — not 2000. This means that millions of mainframe computers, software, and embedded chips that use date/time for calculations will go haywire at 12:00 midnight on January 1, 2000 (a Saturday). They will either shut down or produce bad data, unless they are repaired or replaced before December 31, 1999.

Accurate computer dates are extremely important in today's world because they determine whether people will receive Social Security, pensions, Medicare, retirement benefits, driver's licenses, voter registration, salary increases, tax payments or refunds, seniority benefits, overtime, credit cards, etc.

Computer dates are used in industry to control manufacturing processes and maintenance schedules, and to keep track of machine operations. Financial institutions use computer dates to calculate interest due dates, delinquent accounts, bonuses, commissions, mortgages, bills, loans, and stocks.

In military and commercial navigational systems, tracking time is absolutely essential. Without accurate timing, the computerized navigational systems on trains, airlines, missiles, ships and submarines, or in satellites or nuclear power plants will either malfunction, give erroneous information (with potential catastrophic results), or crash.

The sheer scope of finding and changing all the

affected software and hardware is mind-boggling. In software, hundreds of billions of lines of computer code must be searched manually (that is, line by line) to find the affected date fields. In hardware, the billions of "embedded" chips must first be located. Documentation regarding chip location, however, is often poor or nonexistent. And once found, the "fix" is very complicated.

Software

The complexities of the Y2K fix are multiplied by many variables. For instance, approximately 500 computer languages have been used over the last 40 years. Most of these languages must communicate with each other across networks. Any changes to software programs potentially affect these interactions. Most of the mainframe computers were programmed with COBOL, an outdated (obsolete) computer language that very few of today's younger programmers know or use.

U.S. government computer experts estimate that an additional 500,000 to 700,000 experienced COBOL programmers are needed to make the repairs. They are not available. And there is another problem. The typical large mainframe computer system uses other arcane languages as well. In some systems, there are 20 or more languages, but today hardly anyone understands them. Like COBOL, many of these languages have been out of use for over 20 years.

Moreover, the number of lines of code that must be changed manually is huge. It is not unusual for a company to have 100 million lines of code in the computers they use. Chase Manhattan Bank uses 200 million lines of code. Each one of those lines has to be individually examined to determine if changes are necessary. Chase is spending over $200 million to solve its Y2K problem. Citicorp uses 400 million lines of code; AT&T uses 500 million lines of code; Bank of Boston (the U.S.'s 15th largest bank) uses 60 million lines of code; Social Security uses 67 million lines of code; the IRS uses 100 million lines of code; the Defense Department uses 358 million lines (the latest estimates range up to 1 to 2 billion lines).

Embedded Chips

And if the computer software problem isn't enough, the same Y2K problem also affects our embedded-chip technologies. These systems have enabled us to effectively shrink computers into hand-held devices or components. Many of the approximately 40 billion embedded chips in use today are hardwired with an internal clock that governs its computational uses. It is estimated that 5 percent to 10 percent of these chips are not Y2K compliant. These defective chips and their circuit board must be located and replaced.

Because of their small size and weight, embedded chips tend to be in hard-to-reach places. For example, there are embedded chips at the bottom of oil rigs (some at the bottom of the ocean) that control the flow of oil out of the well. Embedded chips are also located in our satellite systems, including our Global Positioning Satellite (GPS) System, upon which most navigational computation relies (including commercial airlines). The U.S. trucking industry also relies on the GPS satellite system, as does the entire U.S. military.

Embedded chips are also found closer to home. From VCRs, electronic stoves, microwave ovens, watches, alarm clocks, digital phone systems and TVs to sewage pumps, water systems, electrical transforming equipment, traffic signals, credit card readers and ATMs, these chips have permeated every facet of our lives.

TheY2K Risk to America's Infrastructure

The National Power Grid

The national power grid (a complex matrix of public power utilities, dams, and nuclear power plants) is completely computer dependent and may be America's most important system at risk.

"There will be facilities where they go in and turn on the machines and they won't go on," says Dean Kothmann, head of the technology division at the engineering firm Black & Veatch, the world's largest provider of power plants (*Business Week* [March 2, 1998]).

Every participant in the grid must be Y2K compliant if the whole system is to be compliant. If 20 percent of the grid goes down, it could pull down the rest of the grid with it, giving us the "mother of all electrical blackouts." A major depression, social upheaval in American cities, widespread food shortages, and a "state of national emergency" would be only a few of the results of such a failure.

Nuclear power plants, of course, pose an especially worrisome problem. While their basic safety systems should continue to work, other important systems could malfunction because of the Y2K bug. According to Jared S. Wermiel, the man leading the Y2K effort at the Nuclear Regulatory Commission (NRC), in one Y2K test the security computer at a nuclear power plant failed by opening vital areas that are normally locked for security. For that reason, the NRC issued a letter requesting confirmation from utilities that their plants will operate safely on January 1, 2000. Given the complexity and the need to test repaired computers, "it wouldn't surprise me if certain plants find that they are not Year 2000 ready and have to shut down," says Wermeil (*Business Week* [March 2, 1998]).

Railroads at Risk

U.S. railroads, which transport the lion's share of American food, fuels, raw materials, and manufactured goods are now 100 percent computer dependent. Computers guide actual train movements and tell management where the millions of rail cars are located.

The Y2K crisis could easily paralyze the U.S. railroads and hence, the U.S. economy. With the railroads and trucking industry thrown into confusion and gridlock, food deliveries to American cities would halt and grocery shelves would be bare within 72 hours.

The Financial Systems at Risk

In other publications I have analyzed in some detail the emerging global financial crisis (now greatly exacerbated by the Asian financial meltdown), the fragility of the entire global financial system (including our own), the vulnerability of the $125 trillion global-debt pyramid (which includes $56 trillion in highly speculative, highly computerized derivatives), and the potential for a crash in the highly overpriced U.S. stock market, mutual funds market, and the U.S. bond market.

A number of triggers could implode this gargantuan debt/paper pyramid: rising interest rates, political scandals, a Middle East war, massive foreign dumping of U.S. Treasury debt, a collapse of the U.S. dollar, the Asian financial meltdown, etc. The system is fragile. Nonetheless, the most dangerous of all such triggers could be the Y2K crisis. It could trigger a wholesale U.S. and global run on the banks and a stampede into cash and gold, a collapse in the U.S. securities markets and the onset of the biggest global depression since the 1930s (if not bigger). It could also bring about political and social turmoil (especially in major cities).

On September 9, 1997, the central bankers of the G-10 (the top 10 industrialized countries) met in Basel, Switzerland and issued a statement warning of the potential for chaos and an international banking-system failure: "The year 2000 issue is potentially the biggest challenge ever faced by the financial industry. Weak links could pose a risk even to banks and businesses whose computer systems are functioning smoothly."

Again, on November 18, 1997, the Basel Committee on Banking Supervision issued a statement saying, "This issue (Y2K) carries tremendous risks of disruption in the operation of financial institutions (i.e., banks, securities firms, and insurance companies) and in financial markets. The aim is to encourage financial institutions worldwide to commit urgently the resources necessary to become millennium-compliant in a timely fashion."

The World's Computer Systems Are Highly Interconnected

It must be remembered that the world's computer systems are highly interconnected. A computer virus (or bug) in one system could spread quickly to another system. Let's assume that America's major banks and corporations become 100 percent Y2K compliant (a highly unlikely event) although it is now forecast that half (or more) of small to medium-sized businesses, U.S. government agencies (including IRS and the Defense Department), and local and state governments will not be Y2K compliant by the year 2000.

Even if America fixes its Y2K problem, very few countries in the rest of the world will be compliant. It is axiomatic that infected (noncompliant) computers or software will infect or contaminate clean (or compliant) computers or software.

With the size and scope of the data applications upon which we rely — in business, banking, governments, or personal use — and the speed at which they operate, any corrupt data will infiltrate the system within a short period of time. Tests have concluded that even "fixed" data can be corrupted by interaction with an "unfixed" or "noncompliant" database. The worldwide banking industry alone transfers over $2 trillion each day. Considering all the information transferred regularly between data systems on a worldwide basis, the ramifications are far-reaching.

2

Those Elusive Embedded Computer Chips

The majority of computing processors currently in use do not reside within what would normally be considered a computer (mainframe computers, mini-computers, and personal computers). Embedded computer processors are found in cars, elevators, traffic lights, security systems, phone systems, parking systems, heat and ventilation/air conditioning systems, fax machines, copiers, printers, voice-mail systems, and backup power systems for buildings, mainframes, LANs, and PCs.

There are literally billions of embedded computer chips all over the world. Most are not date-sensitive, but some are, and no one can tell where they all are and how many may fail. As defined by the Institute of Electrical Engineers (IEE), embedded systems are devices used to control, monitor, or assist the operation of equipment or machinery. "Embedded" means they are an integral part of the system. Consequently, a casual observer won't see them, and even skilled technicians might need to examine the operation of a piece of equipment for some time before concluding that it contains an embedded control device.

All embedded devices are computers. A simple embedded system consists of a single microprocessor chip. An embedded chip may be packaged with other chips in what is called an Application-Specific Integrated Circuit (ASIC), a hybrid system whose input comes from a detector or sensor and whose output goes to a switch or activator, which, for example, may start or stop the operation of a machine or control the flow of fuel to an engine by an operating valve.

The chip contains its own instructions, a "burned-in" program. If the chip has its program embedded into it, it cannot be changed by software to make it Y2K compliant. It must be replaced if it is not Y2K compliant.

It is estimated that at least 40 billion chips are presently in use throughout the industrialized western world. Of these, an estimated 7 to 10 percent are noncompliant, and could fail at the turn of the century.

Because no one knows which embedded chips are noncompliant, billions of these chips must be tested, one by one, system by system — a task that is simply not possible to complete between now and the year 2000.

The Universal Use of Embedded Chips

Consider how many times a day you depend on equipment or a system that utilizes an embedded computer chip.

Office Systems and Mobile Equipment

1. Telephone systems, mobile telephones
2. Faxes, copiers

3. Time recording systems

4. Still and video cameras

Building Systems

1. Backup lighting and generators
2. Fire control systems
3. Heating and ventilating systems
4. Elevators, escalators
5. Security systems, security cameras
6. Safes and vaults, door locks

Manufacturing and Process Control

1. Manufacturing plants
2. Water and sewage systems
3. Power stations, power grid systems
4. Oil refineries and related storage facilities
5. Bottling plants
6. Automated factories
7. Simulators
8. Test equipment used to program, maintain, and test control systems

Medical Diagnostics, Monitoring, and Life Support

1. Heart defibrillators, pacemaker monitors, respirators
2. Patient information and monitoring systems
3. Pharmaceutical control and dispensing systems, e.g., infusion pumps
4. X-ray equipment, MRI, CT Scan
5. Dialysis, chemotherapy
6. Lab equipment

Transportation

1. Airplanes, trains, buses, trucks, autos, boats

2. Air traffic control systems
3. Signaling systems, traffic lights
4. Radar systems
5. Ticketing systems/machines
6. Car parking and other meters

Communications Systems

1. Telephone exchange, telephone switches
2. Cable systems
3. Satellites, including Global Positioning System
4. Data switching equipment (X.25, SMDS, Frame Relay, etc.)

Banking, Finance, and Commercial Systems

1. Automated teller systems
2. Credit card systems
3. Point-of-sale systems including scanner/cash systems

Testing and Diagnostic Systems

1. Energy metering
2. Environmental monitoring equipment

Can Embedded Chips Be Fixed?

The task of fixing or repairing or replacing billions of embedded chip systems is mind-boggling. For one thing, there are not enough trained personnel to make the replacement in time. But if there were, first you would have to find the chips and determine if they have a Y2K problem. Engineers have reported finding chips performing the same function in identical equipment, yet some are Y2K compliant, and others are not. Replacing embedded chips isn't easy. Some are customized and hard to duplicate. The manufacturers of some chips are out of business or have been acquired by other companies that do not intend to upgrade an "out-of-print" chip. Replacing chips older than three years is almost impossible because they have a short technical lifespan. These embedded chips are delicately attached to circuit boards in most cases. Both the chip and the circuit board must be replaced to solve the problem.

When Might the Embedded Chips Fail?

In embedded systems, the concern is often with intervals rather than with specific dates. An event might need to occur at 100-day intervals rather than on the fifth day of each month. This implies that some Y2K problems may occur both before and after January 1, 2000, but not necessarily on the date itself. On the other hand, there is a possibility that devices with cycles that are measured in hours and minutes (or even seconds) may be affected by the problem because year numbers are the basis of time calculations. In such systems, the failure may not occur on the stroke of midnight but during the following 24 hours.

As *Computer Weekly News* (May 11, 1997) wrote, "The embedded chip problem is huge — potentially affecting our most critical industrial, medical, and military control systems. These systems keep nuclear cores stable; the oil, gas, water, and electricity flowing; they keep our airliners, missiles, and satellites in the air and on course; they keep intensive care units operating; and our high-tech military armed and mobile."

3

A Warning to Congress: Edward Yardeni's Testimony

Edward Yardeni is the highly respected, widely quoted chief economist of Deutsche Morgan Grenfell, a New York-based global investment banking firm. He was quoted in the *Washington Times* in a front-page article entitled "The New Millennium Could Be a Cyber Night-mare" (October 5, 1997).

> Yardeni and other forecasters on Wall Street (i.e., J.P. Morgan) see dire consequences for the economy and financial markets unless business and government pick up the pace of efforts to re-solve the computer problem. Only about 11 percent of American businesses so far have reprogrammed their systems, while key government agencies such as the IRS and Defense Department admit they have a long way to go.
>
> "The Year 2000 problem is a serious threat to the

global economy," said Yardeni. Otherwise known for his optimism, the closely watched forecaster puts the odds of recession starting in 2000 at 40 percent . . . "Computers are critical to transportation, energy, distribution, payroll, just-in-time manufacturing processes, international trade, delivery of oil supplies, aircraft flying patterns and scheduling — everything is affected by this one . . . The main risk is the domino effect where computer and business failure start out as isolated instances and then spread to other sectors," he said.

Speaking before the Senate Banking, Housing, and Urban Affairs Committee on November 4, 1997, Yardeni testified the following:

> The year 2000 problem (Y2K) is a very serious threat to the U.S. economy. Indeed I believe that it is inevitable that it could disrupt the entire global economy in several ways. If the disruptions are significant and widespread, then a global recession is possible. . . . I believe that all businesses, both incorporated and unincorporated, should be required by a new law to publicly reveal their current quarterly outlays on fixing Y2K. They should also be required to reveal their best- and worst-case projections of such outlays.

> Y2K is a unique business risk that requires unique disclosure requirements. It is a systemic risk that will affect all businesses, all vendors, and all customers (i.e., all of us). It will affect even those who long ago anticipated the problem and expect to be completely ready for the year 2000. In other words,

it is a risk to the well-being of our entire local, national, and global community. We must protect not only the interests of investors, but also the general public.

There are bound to be Y2K problems that disrupt all of our lives. Our system of self-interested capitalism is not designed to handle system-wide, indeed global, risk to our collective well-being. If we don't get more information soon, then we risk more problems and greater hardships.

One objection is that too much information might panic the public. Perhaps, if we all panic a bit now, we can minimize the disruptions two years from now. The public may be relatively uninformed and unconcerned about Y2K now, but they are bound to become increasingly anxious as the millennium date approaches.

I have spent the past six months collecting as much information as possible on Y2K. Based on what I know so far, I believe there is a 40 percent risk of a worldwide recession that will last at least 12 months starting in January 2000, and it could be as severe as the 1973–74 global recession. That severe downturn was caused by the OPEC oil crisis, which is a useful analogy for thinking about the potential economic consequences of Y2K. Just as oil is a vital resource for our global economy, so is information. If the supply of information is disrupted, many economic activities will be impaired, if not entirely halted.

The problem is time. All the money in the world

will not stop January 1, 2000 from arriving at 3600 seconds per hour. There is not enough time to fix and test all the systems, with billions of lines of software code around the world, that need to be fixed. Many businesses, governments, and organizations have become aware of the Year 2000 problem only recently and may simply run out of time.

Testing is much more time-consuming than repairing noncompliant code. This might not be a problem for some stand-alone systems. However, the majority of software programs are part of a bigger corporate, industrial, national, and even global network. They often depend on input information generated by other programs. They must all remain compatible as they are fixed.

In other words, the sum total of all interdependent computer systems must all be compliant. The network is the computer. A problem in one system could trigger a domino effect, which poses a great risk to all who fail to test whether their local compliant system is compatible with their global networks. The networks that must function perfectly, at the risk of partial and even total failure, include:

1. Electrical power systems;
2. Telecommunications;
3. Transportation;
4. Manufacturing;
5. Retail and wholesale distribution;
6. Finance and banking;
7. Government services and administration (including taxation);

8. Military defense;

9. International trade.

In other words, the Y2K virus has infected all the vital organs of our global body. It must be removed from all of them. A failure in any one system could corrupt other systems. Most obvious would be a serious disruption in the supply of electricity. The year 2000 problem will be a nonevent only if the global network is fixed 100 percent. Undoubtedly, much will be fixed in time. But there is no doubt that some significant fraction will not be ready in time.

Indeed, most so-called embedded microchip systems will be stress-tested for the first time under real world conditions starting at midnight on New Year's Eve 2000. There are billions of these mini-computers embedded in appliances, elevators, security systems, processing and manufacturing plants, medical devices, and numerous other vital applications. Most are probably not date-sensitive. But many are, and could seriously disrupt vital economic activities and create serious safety hazards.

No one has a "silver-bullet" solution that can fix Y2K over a weekend. They can help to find and repair code that is not Y2K compliant. But every change requires time-consuming testing of each system. Each change has the potential of creating a new bug in the repaired program, which then requires another round of "debugging" and testing. There is simply no silver bullet for this process.

I am amazed by the lack of concern about Y2K by our political and business leaders, journalists, and the general public. The widespread mantra I hear over and over again is "Bill Gates will fix it." The official position of Microsoft is that this is a problem that everyone must fix on his own. It is too big and overwhelming for even Microsoft.

The lack of concern may also reflect the fact that we have become very dependent on technology in a very short period of time in the last 20 years. We depend on it, but very few of us understand how it works and its limitations. We marvel at the achievements of technology. But it doesn't always work as expected and as promised.

Anyone who owns a PC has experienced the frustration of unexpected crashes. Most PCs work fine as long as we don't add any new programs. As soon as we do so, other programs sometimes misbehave. None of us would be happy if our PC was 95 percent functional. So why are we so complacent about a global computer network that might be 95 percent Y2K compliant in a best-case scenario and maybe only 50 percent compliant in a worst-case scenario?

Software programming is far less disciplined and rigorous than most of us realize. Two different programmers can and do write completely different programs that will perform exactly the same task. Programming is more of an art than a science. One of the biggest Y2K headaches is that few programmers take the time or are even asked to document the logic of their programs. Also, the original source code for many older programs is lost. The source code was translated into "machine language," that is, the binary combinations of zeros and ones that computers understand, by so-called "compiler" programs. Reverse compiling is possible, but many of the original compiler programs are also lost.

On Wall Street we have focused our research efforts on how to make money on Y2K. I think it is time for all of us to focus more on the disruptions that may occur because the problem will not be completely fixed in time. There are plausible worst-case disruption scenarios that would undoubtedly cause a global recession, possibly one of the longest and deepest on record. With so much at risk, we must do more to prepare for possible troubles. To do so, we need answers; we need more Y2K disclosure from our business community. Then we can prepare for the worst, and thereby realistically hope for the best.

4

The Extent of the Y2K Crisis

There's no point in sugarcoating the problem. If we don't fix the century-date problem, we will have a situation scarier than the average disaster movie you might see on a Sunday night. Twenty one months from now there could be 90 million taxpayers who won't get their refunds, and 95 percent of the revenue stream of the United States could be jeopardized.

> — IRS commissioner Charles Rossotti,
> *Wall Street Journal* (April 22, 1998)

This is not a prediction, it is a certainty — there will be serious disruptions in the world's financial services industry . . . It's going to be ugly.

> — *The Sunday Times* (July 19, 1998)

It is a large global disaster in the making . . . President Clinton and Vice President Gore have failed to make the problem a national priority.
— Jerry Josinowski, president of the 14,000-member National Association of Manufacturers, *Orange County Register* (July 1, 1998)

We're having a great time now! Why bother with Y2K? I mean, there's money to be made. You can take over other companies. There's the global marketplace. You know, don't bother me with the Year 2,000 problem, it's just annoying . . . I've got to give you this analogy. This is Titanic America. They went down to the ocean floor and they found the rivets. They brought the rivets up from the Titanic. They cut them in half. They found crystal in the metal. What sank the Titanic was . . . the rivets were defective! Think of computers as the rivets of our global economy. They're defective. And we're going full speed at night, in the middle of the Atlantic where it's freezing cold, and everything is brittle, straight for an iceberg. And we're dancing in steerage and having first-class meals on top.
— Dr. Edward Yardeni, chief economist at Deutsche Morgan Grenfell Investment Bankers, at a June 2, 1998, symposium on the Y2K problem

We have to act like Paul Revere, but instead of crying out that "the British are coming," we must warn the people that "the Year 2000 Problem is coming — get ready, take precautions." There's going to be a significant economic disruption. What we are saying is that the problem is real and extremely serious.

— Senator Bob Bennett (R-UT), chairman of the
Senate Committee on the Year 2000 Problem
(May 22, 1998)

The Y2K/millennium bug crisis has definitely gotten increasing amounts of mainline media coverage. Some reports are telling it like it is, some are denying that there really is much of a problem ("it is minor and easily solvable"), and some are actually attacking the "Y2K fanatics" and "doomsayers." A number of articles have appeared saying that "an easy fix has been discovered, not to worry, the problem will soon be solved."

These so-called "easy fixes" are creative programs that will speed up code remediation for certain mainframe computers for certain applications. They will probably have a positive impact on up to 20 percent of the total Y2K problem. In other words, they have limited application for most computer systems, and they have nothing to do with the huge embedded-chip problem or 300 million PCs. But the good news is, some of these new programs will help certain companies to speed up their work. However, they are not "silver bullets" — nor do the experts expect a silver bullet to appear.

Recent polls indicate that a growing number of people in grassroots America are beginning to wake up to the significance of the Y2K problem. It is interesting that working-class Americans earning less than $30,000 per year are more concerned than more affluent respondents who believe that government and business will solve the problem rather easily. It is safe to say that we are finally beginning to move into the "public awareness stage."

Within a few months, this will become the "growing concern stage," then the "deep concern stage," and finally — perhaps in six to nine months — the "panic stage." Meanwhile, most corporate managers and most politicians are still in the "complacency/denial stage."

However, not all corporate leaders are complacent or in denial. Some of the wealthiest, top-ranking Wall Street and corporate executives are not selling their stocks "like there was no tomorrow," while concurrently seducing the public to "buy, buy, buy on the way to 15,000." It does seem hypocritical, but from their point of view, they have to have someone to sell their stocks to (the suckers). It happened that way in 1929 shortly before the crash. So on Wall Street and around the country, we are presently entering the "big money is bailing out (BMIBO) stage."

In order to keep middle-class Americans and their retirement/savings funds fully invested in the stock market long enough to let the big guys get their money out, the controlled, mainline financial media must continue to hype the economy and play down the millennium bug crisis and the Asian financial crisis. In addition, they must denigrate those who are warning of the Y2K crisis and calling for preparedness. They or their establishment bosses don't want to contribute to a panic (not yet, at any rate) by writing too negatively about Y2K. They can't have a panic until the big guys are out. That is why the media have, for the most part, played down Y2K!

The July 7, 1998 issue of *USA Today* carried a feature article in its finance section entitled "Breakthrough May Help to Squash Year 2000 Bug," which said, "A new tool to fix the Year 2000 problem may be a breakthrough that could speed the government, banks, and companies toward a solution." The article, however, failed to point out that the "new tool" only had limited application for a limited number of computers in a limited number of companies.

Steve Forbes' Call to Arms

On May 13, 1998, Steve Forbes (chairman of the highly respected *Forbes* magazine and candidate for president in 1996) issued the following warning regarding Y2K in a memorandum to every member of Congress:

> The Year 2000 (Y2K) computer crisis is now upon us and the federal government is even more woefully unprepared than the rest of society. The implications are ominous. Medicare, the IRS, the Federal Aviation Administration and other basic agencies are operating on utterly out-of-date technology. It doesn't take much imagination to see how dreadfully wrong things could go.

> Some Y2K problems have surfaced already, more will surface soon. Most states begin their fiscal 2000 years on July 1, 1999; the federal government, on October 1, 1999.

> "There is very little realization that there will be a disruption," Sherry Burns, director of the Central Intelligence Agency's office studying the Year 2000 problem, told *Reuters*. "As you start getting out into the population, I think most people are again assuming that things are going to operate the way they always have. That is not going to be the case."

> "There is no way we're going to fix 100 percent of all the computer systems around the world in

time," warned Edward Yardeni, chief economist with Deutsche Morgan Grenfell, in an April interview with the technology magazine, *FORBES ASAP*. "My analogy is the 1973-74 recession. Just the way a disruption in the supply of oil caused a global recession, a disruption in the flow of information, especially if it is critically important information, might similarly disrupt global economic activity and produce a recession."

The federal government's Y2K compliance efforts recently received a "D-minus" grade by the House Subcommittee on Government Management, Information and Technology, chaired by Representative Steve Horn of California.

What has the Administration's technology point man, Vice President Al Gore, been doing for the past five years? . . . At its core, this is not a technology crisis; it is a leadership crisis.

We have the technology to fix or replace every computer and software program affected by Y2K, though it will be expensive. Technical corrections are estimated to cost between $300 billion and $600 billion globally. Litigation, lost business, and bankruptcies could drive the costs over $1 trillion.

Distracted by scandals and side-tracked by questionable crises like global warming, the Clinton–Gore Administration is failing to ensure that vital government computers will be fixed in time. Nor are they impressing the American public and foreign governments with the urgency of this crisis. Why such silence? Are they trying to limit public concern until after the mid-term elections? The stakes are too high for such partisan political games.

With the Clinton–Gore Administration AWOL, Congress must urgently fill this leadership vacuum. It must increase defense funding to speed up compliance. Create Y2K compliance penalties and incentives for key federal agencies. Require the Federal Emergency Management Agency (which itself received a "D-minus" grade for Y2K compliance) to develop contingency plans for major disruptions in vital services. Move fast. Time is short.

Many of Steve Forbes' concerns were validated by President Clinton's Y2K czar, John Koskinen, in an address that tried to play down the Clinton inactivity on the Y2K crisis:

Only 63 percent of the 7,850 federal computer systems deemed "mission critical" — that is, vital to protecting U.S. national security, health, safety, education, transportation, and financial and emergency management — will be ready on January 1, 2000.

Five Cabinet-level departments (Defense, Education, Transportation, Labor and State) received 'F' grades. Only 24 percent of Defense's mission-critical systems have been fixed to date. Only 36 percent are expected to be fixed by 1 January, 2000. At this rate, Defense's mission-critical systems won't be completely fixed until 2009.

"The impact of [Year 2000 computer] failures could

be widespread, costly, and potentially disruptive to military operations worldwide," concluded a chilling April 1998 General Accounting Office report. "In an August 1997 operational exercise, the Global Command and Control System failed testing when the date was rolled over to the Year 2000. GCCS is deployed at 700 sites worldwide and is used to generate a common operating picture of the battlefield for planning, executing, and managing military operations. The U.S., and its allies . . . would be unable to orchestrate a Desert Storm-type engagement in the Year 2000 if the problem is not corrected."

Serious problems face the private sector, too. According to a March 1998 survey by the Information Technology Association of America and The Y2K Group:

94 percent of Information Technology managers see the Y2K computer issue as a "crisis"

44 percent of American companies have already experienced Y2K computer problems

83 percent of U.S. Y2K transition project managers expect the Dow Jones Industrial Average to fall by at least 20 percent as the crisis begins to unfold.

5

Why America Will Not Be Ready for Y2K

Most Americans who have heard of theY2K crisis don't understand the problem, its all-encompassing scope, or its implications. In fact, most U.S. businesses have barely begun to work seriously on the problem. Only 11 percent of companies had reprogrammed their systems as of October 1997. Most federal, state, and local governments are way behind schedule in becoming Y2K compliant before the December 31, 1999, target date. The same can be said for European and Asian businesses and banks.

The Clinton administration has, to date, publicly ignored the crisis; Wall Street has played it down in order to perpetuate investor enthusiasm for buying its stocks and bonds; the mainline media have minimized Y2K; and certain large publications like the *Los Angeles Times* have actually ridiculed commentators who warned of the severity of the crisis.

The *Los Angeles Times* (November 3, 1997) carried a

front-page article entitled "Debunking Year 2000's Computer Disaster," and subtitled "Computer System Disaster Warnings Called Largely Hype." The *Times* accused those who have been warning about the crisis of "playing chicken little" and of trying to profit from the crisis by selling books, compliance services, etc.

Why People Deny the Evidence That Y2K is Real

In his newsletter, *Personal Update* (January 1998), Chuck Missler wrote an article entitled "The Coming Computer Crisis." In a section entitled "Dealing With Disbelief," Missler wrote, "Many have likened our dealing with this issue to the phases of adjustment one goes through in the death of a loved one. The most immediate phase is denial . . . What is clear is that the majority of people, when dealing with Y2K, retreat quickly into denial once the scope and its implications are realized. Time is running out — both for those working directly on Y2K projects and those preparing for the possible consequences. There simply is no time for denials."

A recent survey of 108 companies across 14 industries by Cap Gemini, a computer consulting firm, found that only one in six Fortune 500 companies "has implemented a full-fledged plan for year 2000 compliance." Another survey by the research/consulting firm, the Gartner Group, found that 40 percent of companies "have not progressed beyond the initial awareness and assessment phase of the crisis . . . We're projecting 30 percent of organizations will have mission-critical systems failures." The awareness assessment phase of a Y2K project is only 1–5 percent of the completed repair project.

According to another survey, only 33 percent of

companies nationwide have a detailed plan in place to deal with the code-correction program and 7 percent of the companies have already suffered some kind of date code-related problem or failure.

As of the end of 1997, there was not one Fortune 500-size company that was compliant, even though some had been working on Y2K repairs for five years. There is no evidence that a large company can solve the problem in two, three, or even five years. Purdue University and Oklahoma State University have been working on it since 1985, and neither is presently compliant.

Leon Kappelman, a computer systems professor at the University of North Texas and co-chairman of a year-2000 working group of the International Society of Information Management, has talked to people in the trenches and doesn't like what he hears.

"At this point, we have so much work to do we can't possibly get it done," said Kappelman, who periodically surveys the society's membership of 2,700 information technology managers, academics, and consultants to get a sense of what companies and agencies are actually doing to solve the problem.

From his most recent survey, Kappelman estimates that between 25–40 percent of the nation's companies and agencies are doing "real work." Between 35–50 percent aren't doing anything, and the rest are still "planning."

Major consulting, research, and investment-analyst firms generally agree that time has run dangerously short. Most informed computer consultants believe that it will take a minimum of two to three years to find, assess, test, and repair computers.

"I'm not a doomsayer at all," says Bob Austrian, an

analyst at the investment bank NationsBanc Montgomery Securities in San Francisco, "But when I see an ad in the *Wall Street Journal* in November 1997 from the Los Angeles International Airport looking for bids just to assess its year 2000 needs, I sit and wonder."

The federal government is even further behind in Y2K compliance than business and industry. As of late 1997, according to the quarterly report of the U.S. Office of Management and Budget, "Progress on Year 2000 Conversion," 18 of the 25 major government agencies are planning to implement their Y2K solutions during the last three months of 1999. As of November 1997, the House Congressional Sub-Committee on Government Management, Information, and Technology gave eight U.S. government agencies "D's" on their preparation for Y2K. These include the IRS; the Departments of Energy, Health and Human Services; Agriculture; Education; and Transportation.

The Office of Management and Budget (OMB) has found 8,589 mission-critical systems (excluding the Social Security Administration, which has identified 29,139 modules). Of this total, 13 percent must be replaced and 62 percent must be repaired. Of the 5,332 mission-critical systems that are to be repaired, only 2 percent are fixed and working, 5 percent are fixed and have been tested, and 12 percent are fixed and being tested.

In congressional testimony given on July 10, 1997, Joel C. Willemson, the director of Information Resources Management of the Accounting and Information Management Division of the U.S. General Accounting Office (GAO), warned that federal agencies are running out of time to prepare for the millennium. He stated that the OMB's compliance efforts are highly inadequate and that the majority of federal agencies will miss their December 31, 1999 deadlines for Y2K compliance.

Reasons Why Business and Government Will Not Be Y2K Compliant by the Year 2000

1) The Y2K Project is the Largest Computer Repair Project in History

There is less than one year to complete computer repairs. We simply don't have enough time or computer programmers to finish the job. Furthermore, many studies show that over 80 percent of normal software repair projects are not completed on time. The Y2K project simply was started too late, and time is quickly running out.

2) The Size and Cost of the Y2K Compliance Project Have Been Grossly Underestimated

The original cost estimates (by the Gartner Group) for "fixing" the Y2K problem were $300 to $600 billion. But if you figure that individual companies (or banks, like Citicorp, Chase Manhattan, Merrill Lynch, etc.) are spending $200 million (or more) each, the final cost is likely to be in the trillions of dollars. Technology Management Reports (a San Diego-based research firm) now estimates that the cost will exceed $2 trillion. Moreover, the cost of correcting each line of code is rising from $1.30 per line in late 1997 to $4.00 per line by the year 2000, as companies and governments get desperate and compete for a very short supply of competent programmers (who are familiar with COBOL and FORTRAN).

The scope of the Y2K crisis has also been grossly underestimated. Business and governments tended to focus on the old mainframes and ignored the 275 million personal computers (PCs) and the 40 billion embedded microchips worldwide that are also infected with the Y2K bug.

3) There Are Not Enough Experienced Programmers to Fix the Problem

Today, there are about 500,000 programmers in business, industry, and government working on the day-to-day running of these computer systems. Only a small portion of these programmers can be released to work on Y2K problems. We need an additional 500,000–700,000 high-tech, trained programmers competent in COBOL and dozens of other outdated languages to change hundreds of billions of lines of code manually — one line at a time. Such programmers simply do not exist in the numbers that are needed in the time remaining.

In *Remnant Review* (February 1, 1997), Gary North wrote about the shortage of experienced programmers:

> British Telecom has now budgeted about $600 million to fix its Y2K problem. At an average salary of $50,000 a year, this means that the company will hire some 5,000 programmers for 2.5 years. At $30,000 a year, that's 8,000 programmers. Think about this. Just one company. Meanwhile, the shortage of skilled mainframe programmers in Britain is now estimated to be around 33,000.
>
> AT&T has 500 million lines of code to go through. The typical programmer can go through about 100,000 lines a year and fix any bad lines. So, AT&T needs around 5,000 programmers (deadline for testing: 12/98). At the same rate of repair, Citicorp

(400m lines) needs 4,000. Chase Manhattan (200m lines) needs 2,000. And so on. Do you think a Fortune 500-level company can go down to Manpower this week and hire an extra 5,000 mainframe programmers with experience — no pension, no guaranteed job beyond 2001 — as "temps"?

Where will any nation find tens of thousands of skilled mainframe programmers who are not already engaged in keeping existing systems going? Some 90-day COBOL wonder can't do the work. In a multimillion-line system, there may be 10 other languages used besides COBOL. One researcher recently identified a system with 70 languages in its programs. The temps must be familiar with these other languages, too. Forget it. It's impossible.

I spoke with a programmer who wrote part of the Medicaid system. He told me, "We were on a tight schedule. I used every language I could find to help me. I was told to do it with COBOL only, but my supervisor knew I was breaking the rules. We were all breaking the rules. I used at least a dozen different languages. I didn't write up any documentation for this, so there is no way that anyone coming in now will know what I did. I just wrote code."

For three decades, the best and the brightest of the programmers "just wrote code." They did not write documentation — i.e., summaries or manuals. Those who now must piece together what those genius programmers did decades ago have less than two years to get it done, ready for testing. It's impossible.

4) There Are Few Manuals to Explain Previously Performed Code Work

The code/programming work was done by different people (in many different languages over the years) who provided very little (if any) documentation as to what was done or how.

5) Very Few Companies or Local Governments Had Begun Implementing a Y2K Program

It is primarily the large Fortune 500-type companies (with huge resources), large banks, and Wall Street brokerage firms, and certain federal government agencies that will meet the deadline for Y2K compliance. Fifty to 75 percent of small- to medium-sized companies will be unable to do so, nor will the great majority of local or state governments. The governor of New York has declared Y2K compliance for his state government to be a top priority, but that is an exception.

6. Testing of the Repairs Will Take More Time Than Most Companies Have

Between 40-70 percent of the Y2K project must be devoted to testing, which can take six to twelve months to iron out the bugs. But as computer consultant Capers Jones has said, the testing will not be done by more than a handful of organizations because most will never finish their actual code repair before December 31, 1999. In his widely respected report, Jones says that any organization that had not begun its code repair by October 1997, will not complete its project. However, by October 1997, less than 20 percent of the Fortune 500 corporations had begun repairing the code.

Moreover, parallel testing is mandatory for large systems (systems having 10 million lines or more). Data must be fed into the noncompliant machine and compliant machine simultaneously in order to make sure the compliant machine handles the data properly. Such testing can go on for weeks or months. To run these parallel tests, an organization needs excess mainframe computer capacity of 100 percent, but most mainframes are already running at capacity. This means that most corporations that complete their repairs will be unable to fully test their repaired Y2K systems because very little mainframe capacity is available.

7) The Main Y2K Problem Will Be Compounded by Interdependent Systems Failures

Those who have completed their work will be impacted by those who don't because noncompliant computers and data will corrupt those that are compliant.

8) Despite Media Reports, PCs (Personal Computers) Are Also Infected

The *Chicago Tribune* wrote an article entitled "Look Out PCs, Here Comes Your Y2K Crisis" (September 30, 1997) that quoted a speech given by British computer consultant Karl Feilder at the SPG Year 2000 Conference entitled "If You Can Sleep Properly at Night, You Don't Understand the Significance of the PC Problem." Feilder said, "The PC problem is horrendous. We conducted the largest-ever independent testing of PC programs and hardware. We have tested the Basic Input/Output System, or BIOS, on over 500 types of PCs, and of those machines made before 1997, 93 percent failed the BIOS test. This is very real and will have a far-reaching effect."

Ninety-three percent of PCs manufactured before January 1993 have Y2K problems.

Feilder explained that since 1984, personal computers have stored data on an embedded chip called the RTC (real time clock). The real-time clock tells your computer the day, time, and year in two-digit expressions.

"We have tested 4,000 PC programs," said Feilder. "Only 28 percent claimed to be Y2K compliant; 4.4 percent didn't know that 2000 is a leap year; 3.5 percent only work in the 20th century; and 11.5 percent store dates different from the user input. There is, however, encouraging news. Of the computers that have come out in 1997, we're finding that only 47 percent fail. Of course, if only 47 percent of the world's PCs fail, it's still a pretty serious problem, but at least it's encouraging.

"I think that this problem is going to be far worse than anyone expects," said Feilder. "PCs are full of programs, they're full of software, they're full of hardware bits, and one or each part of these can have Year 2000 problems. Worse still, most companies haven't begun to even assess the problem. I'm taking bookings into the middle of next year for awareness programs. What am I going to tell them? 'Hey, guys, wonderful you're here. It's too late!'"

Leon Kappelman, editor of the *Year 2000 Journal*, says that the PC problem has been grossly underreported because the mainframe problem is so large it has received most of the media attention. "Embedded systems in PCs definitely have a problem and it's very, very real," said Kappelman.

Gary North carried the following information on PC compliance on his web site (www.garynorth.com):

There are about 250 million PCs out there. If they run on DOS, they aren't 2000-compliant. If they run on Windows 3x, they aren't 2000-compliant. If they have not had their BIOS chips replaced, they aren't compliant. If they are running any piece of software that is not compliant, they aren't compliant. Think of a spreadsheet that isn't compliant, but which still keeps running . . . wrong.

It is law in the United States that all Internal Revenue Service quarterly payments be submitted by computer in the year 2000. What if these PC computers are not compliant? Most of them won't be. (This won't matter, of course, since the IRS's mainframe computer will not be compliant, either.)

What happens to world productivity when 230 million out of 250 million PCs either shut down or start scrambling their programs? What happens to networks? What happens to insurance companies and banks that rely on PCs to input data?

6

Sudden Impact: The Effect of Y2K on America

Y2K is Threatening Corporate America

John Koskinen, President Clinton's Y2K czar, has defended the government's poor Y2K repair performance by pointing out that corporate America is doing just as poorly. He is probably right. Senator Robert Bennett's Y2K Committee reported in June 1998 that 58 percent of U.S. businesses polled have not even calculated Y2K costs. Fewer than 60 percent of U.S. businesses have even completed preliminary assessments to determine the extent of their problem. The committee concluded that "top corporation remediation efforts fall considerably below levels necessary to avoid severe business disruption."

A poll conducted of 400 chief information officers (CIOs) and chief executive officers (CEOs) of Fortune 500 companies indicated that 70 percent admit they have underestimated the dimension and cost of the problem; over

70 percent of these executives do not believe that repairs will be in place on time, and 50 percent do not yet have a detailed plan in place. More than half of those executives said they are going to avoid commercial airlines and elevators on January 1, 2000.

Most companies have tripled their original estimates of the cost of fixing the Y2K problem. In light of the acute shortages of software programmers, companies have been raiding one another's experts and offering six-figure salaries to the programmers. There are 340,000 qualified people in the world qualified to do the job, according to Peter de Jager, and twice that number are desperately needed.

The Gartner Group, an industry consulting company, expects about a 30 percent business failure rate worldwide due to Y2K. If accurate, this failure of 30 percent of U.S. corporations would produce millions of layoffs and staggering financial losses. Many experts are predicting that at least half of America's small- to medium-sized companies will not be Y2K compliant by December 31, 1999.

Fear of Lawsuits Slowing Down Y2K Repair

One of the problems with fixing corporate America's computers is that outside computing consultant firms are now beginning to refuse to take work for fear that they might be sued if the client company doesn't complete its Y2K repairs or if it experiences computer malfunctions despite Y2K compliance efforts. Many of these large consulting firms (including IBM and EDS) will take on no new clients because of the danger of liability lawsuits. In an article entitled "Consultants Shunning Work on Year 2000" (June 29, 1998), the *Wall Street Journal* reported the following:

The consulting arms of several big accounting firms, fearing lawsuits, are refusing to fix year 2000 computer problems or offering to do so only for certain clients.

Many computer consultants initially jumped at the chance to rewrite old computer code or convert computer systems to use new code that acknowledges the year 2000. But an increasing number are shunning the work because "they're afraid of being sued," says Larry Martin, president of Data Dimensions, Inc., a computer consulting company in Bellevue, Washington.

Just listen to Carl Sellberg, top technology partner at Coopers & Lybrand. "We don't do year 2000 work other than to warn existing clients that they may have a problem," he said, adding: "There's a great deal of risk of litigation."

Deloitte & Touche's top consulting partner Pat Loconto says his firm isn't soliciting new clients for year 2000 work because the firm doesn't want to be viewed as a deep pocket in potential lawsuits.

The legal departments in many companies are now telling employees not to reveal any information on the status of their Y2K repairs to customers or the public for fear of lawsuits. So, as everyone clams up about their Y2K progress, and consultants back away from fixing business computers for fear of lawsuits, we are flying blind, and the whole Y2K repair process in corporate America will slow down dramatically.

The Danger of "Just in Time" Inventory Systems

Chuck Missler wrote the following analysis in his *Personal Update* newsletter (July 1998):

In the last 15 years, the manufacturing sector has revolutionized their industry with "just in time" inventorying, thus eliminating large reserves of necessary resources, and greatly reducing the associated costs.

Because of the success of this philosophy, almost every industry worldwide has adopted some variation of it. No longer are there vast reserves of medical supplies in hospitals, car parts for assembly, or replacement parts for power-generating facilities. This adds to the fragility of not only manufacturing systems, but financial and information systems as well.

Multiple markets worldwide are strung tight. It only takes a small blip to impede normal operations. These systems are built one upon another like a house of cards. Each one is part of a three-dimensional construction, dependent on the others for smooth transference of information or resources. There are no safety nets of supplies to ride out unexpected events. The phenomenon of failure across systems is called "the ripple effect."

Software programmers are acutely aware of this effect. Frequently a seemingly small program change will cause an unpredictable side effect in some other portion of the project. This is one of the complicating features of this task. As the programs are adjusted for the date problem, the programmers themselves often create unpredictable errors.

Like a pebble dropped into a quiet pool, a single failure can radiate out to touch other "shores." And as multiple pebbles dropped into the same pool, the radiating ripples interact with other ripples until it is impossible to count both the interactions and their effects on the shore they reach.

The Y2K Impact on the Automobile Industry

Ralph J. Szygendon, chief information officer at General Motors, made the following statement in *Fortune* magazine (April 27, 1998): "At each one of our factories there are catastrophic problems. Amazingly enough, machines on the factory floor are far more sensitive to incorrect dates than we ever anticipated. When we tested robotic devices for transition into the year 2000, for example, they just froze and stopped operating."

General Motors is the largest manufacturing company in the world. It used to be said that what is good for General Motors is good for the country and vice-versa, but today General Motors is in trouble for three reasons: 1) it is a long way from having its Y2K problems fixed and tested; 2) most of its 100,000 suppliers are not Y2K compliant; and 3) the last United Auto Workers strike devastated the company, its suppliers, and the city of Detroit and other towns where GM plants or its supplier plants are located.

When the CIO of General Motors says there are "catastrophic problems in every GM plant," it is worth taking note. According to the *Fortune* article, GM and the other auto companies are very highly dependent on embedded processors. The article cited an experiment at a GM plant to evaluate its risk. When the plant engineers advanced their computer clocks to the year 2000, the plant was instantly incapacitated, as robotic devices froze in mid-air.

When Chrysler Corporation shut down its Sterling Heights assembly plant last year and turned all the plant's clocks to December 31, 1999, executives expected to find computer glitches associated with the date change from 1999 to 2000. But they didn't expect quite so many glitches. "We got lots of surprises," said Chrysler chairman Robert Eaton. "Nobody could get out of the plant. The security system absolutely shut down and wouldn't let anybody in or out. And you obviously couldn't have paid people, because the time-clock systems didn't work."

Y2K Risk from Corporate Suppliers

Ask year 2000 project managers what keeps them up at night and chances are you'll get the same answers: suppliers.

Virtually all large companies rely on hundreds, if not thousands, of external hardware and software vendors, utilities, banks, transportation companies, and other service providers. A date-conversion Y2K problem at any single point in those supply chains could bring a business to its knees.

Some companies, such as Nabisco, have adopted a "trust but verify" approach toward suppliers. Other companies are still surveying suppliers about their year 2000 plans and determining which suppliers are most critical to them. General Motors has 100,000 suppliers, including 13,000 first-tier direct suppliers. The company sent out questionnaires to their suppliers and asked for quarterly reports on their Y2K compliance efforts. Much to their surprise, only 26 percent of the suppliers responded. Consequently, General Motors trained 150–200 auditors to go to the suppliers to ascertain their status of Y2K compliance. The auditors discovered that most of the suppliers are not Y2K compliant; moreover, many do not even have a plan. In short, they are in denial.

Even assuming GM's major suppliers were Y2K compliant, how compliant are those suppliers' suppliers? A chain reaction of noncompliance from supplier to supplier to supplier to GM (or Ford or Chrysler) can shut down the auto industry even if the Big Three (who are spending over $1 billion on Y2K) become compliant. It should be kept in mind that each of the major American auto companies have over a billion lines of computer code and hundreds of thousands of chips embedded in their equipment, all of which must be repaired. The chairman of Dana Corp. (a top supplier to GM) recently said that "Y2K is the biggest problem to ever face the U.S. auto industry."

The 1998 General Motors Strike:
An Illustration of the Domino Effect

The recent United States Autoworkers strike against GM caused huge problems. It illustrates the kind of ripple effect that may occur with the Y2K crisis. GM and the UAW were at war. The strike couldn't have come at a worse time. Incredibly, most of GM's suppliers live week to week on very small profit margins. They each have their own "just-in-time systems" in place. The strike occurred at a single stamping plant. Within days 29 auto assembly plants closed. Most of these suppliers (many of which do the lion's share of their business with GM) began shutting down their own factories and laid off up to 80 percent of their work forces prior to the end of the strike.

American Axle, for example, does 86 percent of its business with GM. They closed down due to the strike. Delphi has 90 percent of its business with GM. It closed down. Eregrine (a $1 billion plus company) does all of its business with GM. They laid off 80 percent of their workers due to the strike. GM's suppliers downsized their work forces during the strike by 60–80 percent and many are operated in the red in 1998. How can they afford the big price tag to fix the Y2K problem? They will have to borrow from the banks — that is, if the banks will loan to them in this deflationary environment.

The strike and resulting domino effect severely hurt the local economy of Detroit (and Michigan) as hundreds of thousands of laid-off workers (many of whom live paycheck to paycheck, with no savings) couldn't afford to shop, pay their rent, make mortgage payments. Local doctors, dentists, and businesses couldn't collect on their receivables. Detroit was in such bad shape that a large bank put up signs at all of its teller windows in early July telling people that they could not pull out their deposits in cash.

The Y2K Impact on Small Businesses

Most business and employment in America is still created by small businesses. A survey conducted by Wells Fargo Bank estimates nearly five million U.S. small businesses will face year 2000 computer glitches that could disrupt their businesses. Three-fourths of the businesses surveyed indicated they had done nothing to address the problem. Incredibly, 50 percent said they didn't intend to take action but would wait to see if reports of big problems proved true after January 1, 2000.

The survey of 500 small businesses conducted by the Gallup Organization in April found that 82 percent of those firms surveyed would encounter computer problems and 34 percent could have problems with other equipment that use microchips. The study was conducted for Wells Fargo by the National Federation for Independent Business (NFIB).

The Gartner Group released a study that shows that 84 percent of companies with fewer than 100 employees have done virtually nothing to ensure their computers are Y2K compliant. About one-third of those companies rely heavily enough on computers to expect significant problems at midnight on December 31, 1999, according to Gartner.

William Dennis, senior research fellow at the NFIB Education Foundation, said that more than 330,000 small businesses risk closing their doors until the problem is fixed, and more than 370,000 are likely to be temporarily crippled by year 2000 computer glitches.

"I think there is a sense of security among small businesses because they don't consider their offices to be a technology powerhouse," said Claire McAuliffe, principal of San Francisco-based M2 Inc., a management consulting firm. "But the issue is not what they do inside; it's how they interact with their clients and vendors."

It is sobering to realize that much of our economy is driven by the millions of small businesses that are the most uninformed about the Y2K crisis and the least able financially to deal with it. If the NFIB is correct, and

330,000 small businesses close their doors and another 370,000 are at least temporarily crippled by Y2K, that alone is enough to precipitate a serious depression in America.

The Y2K Impact on Business and the Economy

What happens to the economy if the problem is not resolved by mid-1999? Are corporations and consumers not likely to withhold spending decisions and possibly even withdraw funds from banks if they fear the economy is facing chaos?

— Senator Patrick Moynihan (D-NY) in a letter to President Clinton, July 31, 1996

The crash of 1929 will pale in comparison to the "crash of the century." Layoffs will be rampant, unemployment will rise dramatically, and the economy will drown in dismal depression.

— Investment Counselor Tony Keyes,
Computer World (October 27, 1997)

The Y2K crisis is likely to have a devastating effect on U.S. business, the economy, unemployment, bankruptcies, etc. Capers Jones, a software expert in the Y2K field, estimates that 5–7 percent of U.S. businesses will go bankrupt as a result of year 2000 failures. Robert Rairden, professor of applied computer technology at Illinois State University, says, "Five to 20 percent of businesses faced with fixing their systems will choose not to fix it and close. If 5–20 percent of U.S. business disappears, we've got major problems."

In preparing for this book, I interviewed dozens of computer experts, consultants, and programmers to get their opinion on the Y2K problem. While a few were sanguine, most were not. The consensus of these people is that many of the largest U.S. corporations, banks, and security firms (with huge resources at their disposal) will be Y2K compliant before the deadline.

Most of them also agreed that 50 percent or more of small- to medium-sized businesses, many state and local governments, and a significant number of smaller banks would not be compliant. They also expected that the vast majority (60-80 percent) of businesses and banks in other countries would not be compliant.

The domino effect on American business if even 5–10 percent of businesses were to fail would be catastrophic. Remember, when United Parcel Service (UPS) went on strike last summer for just two weeks, it bankrupted 600 U.S. corporations.

Unemployment will rise sharply in the wake of the Y2K crisis. Even if millions of workers are given a "forced vacation" for only a month or two in early year 2000, it will be an economic disaster for tens of millions of Americans who live from paycheck to paycheck, who have no savings, and who could not survive without a month's pay. As of 1993, 11 percent of all U.S. households had a zero or negative net worth, 15 percent of married couples under 35 years of age had a zero to negative household net worth, and 25 percent had a net worth under $5,000. These families have no cushion if the Y2K crisis should cause temporary layoffs of a few weeks to a few months in early 2000.

If any significant portion of the banks, the power grid, the securities markets, the oil industry, the transportation system, and telecommunications are impacted by the Y2K problem, it will cause a recession in the year 2000. However, if any of these are moderately to severely impacted, the U.S. economy is likely to come crashing down in the worst depression in U.S. history.

The Y2K Impact on the Communications Industry

Phones have become an intimate part of our daily lives. In addition to family communication and Internet access, phones are essential to the survival of most businesses. Banks would be in real trouble should the phone system go down for any appreciable length of time, and the stock markets would die. Every credit card transaction depends upon the phone system for validation. ATMs rely on it as well. Fax transmissions occur over the phone lines. Wide-area networks, used by large corporations and government agencies, rely on phone system assets (like T1 lines) in order to function. The examples are endless. A failure of the national and global telephone networks would leave us all with a severely restricted ability to communicate.

American business and the economy depend on telecommunications, and the U.S. telephone companies depend 100 percent on computers. The phone system is extremely date-sensitive. Because all connections are logged with a date and a time, the telephone industry must look for Y2K problems in the code of the billing software and also in the embedded systems of the network switch and router units.

Computer consultant Karl Feilder recently described the state of Y2K compliance among phone companies around the world. He noted the following:

1) British Telecom is still not prepared to guarantee that the UK phone system will operate uninterrupted into

2000. They have been working on the problem for at least two years and have hundreds of staff directly or indirectly involved in the project. I believe that their publicly stated figure is about 500 million U.S. dollars, but I have been told that the realistic number is a lot higher.

2) Australia's leading telephone provider, Telstra, has increased its publicly stated Y2K budget from 80 million to 400 million U.S. dollars.

3) South Africa's Telkom (still operated as a government monopoly) started its remediation only recently. By their own admission "a comprehensive company-wide year 2000 compliance project was launched in Telkom during January 1997."

4) One United States "Baby Bell" telephone company has over 50,000 PCs that must be checked and made compliant.

They did not start to take inventory until 1998. If British Telecom started in 1995 and is still not sure if they will make it, when will this Baby Bell be ready?

For most businesses, the telephone system is essential to their survival. It is truly the Achilles heel of U.S. business and the economy. If the phone systems go down for days, weeks, or months, many businesses (or most) businesses will not be able to function, many will not survive, and the U.S. economy and financial system will suffer tremendously.

The Y2K Impact on the United States

It has been said that worse than a foreign power hitting America with biological weapons, terrorist attacks, bombs, or missiles would be the taking down of our telephone/telecommunications system — we would collapse overnight. Next to the electric power grid, the second most critical element to the continued functioning of the American economy are telephones and telecommunications. Without these systems up and running, most businesses could not continue. Can Y2K take down America's phone and telecommunications system? Yes, it can! Can failure of the power grid take down the telephone system? Yes, it can!

On May 19, 1998, *USA Today* carried the following article entitled "Year 2000 Bug Threatens Phone Service":

"Make a phone call on January 1, 2000, and there's a good chance that the call won't go through. There's a 50 percent to 60 percent chance each major carrier will suffer at least one failure of a mission-critical system," says Lou Marcoccio, a research director with The Gartner Group. And that's despite the industry spending more than two years and billions of dollars to rid their systems of Year 2000 bugs.

The telecommunications industry trails banks and insurers in fixing Year 2000 problems, making some network trouble inevitable as the millennium nears, experts warn.

Small, mid-size and foreign-based carriers will be affected most. France, Germany, Japan as well as many countries in Southeast Asia, Central Africa and Latin America have spent less time and resources to fix the problem.

U.S. fire and police department dispatch systems are vulnerable, too, the Federal Communications

Commission says. So are many older corporate switchboards, owned and operated by telephone users, not telephone companies.

Telephone networks are computerized at every level, from the transmission of calls to billing and ordering of supplies. Programs throughout the system must be fixed. Every piece of problem equipment must be identified, given a priority, fixed and tested.

"Failures could range from billing problems to a complete lack of phone service. It's impossible to say how widespread they will be or how long they will last," Marcoccio says.

"No one is putting telecommunications companies under the microscope the way bankers are examined," says David Baker, a technology analyst at Schwab Washington Research Group. The Federal Communications Commission can't impose a solution, but it has sent letters to hundreds of companies calling for action. FCC commissioner Michael Powell says, "The vast majority of police and fire equipment is not Year 2000 compliant."

Gartner says big U.S. carriers are spending $70 million to $400 million each to fix their year 2000 problem. AT&T, the largest, expects to spend a total of $463 million on the problem in 1997 and 1998. It has hundreds of people working on the problem full time, says AT&T's John Pasqua.

SBC Communications Group is spending $250 million to fix its year 2000 problem.

The potential legal liabilities are huge. "If some of these systems go down you are going to have a lot of cases," says Steven Brummel, a partner with the Weil Gotshal & Manges office in Brussels, Belgium.

A Major AT&T Glitch

On April 14, 1998, one of AT&T's phone hubs failed because of a reported software problem. This caused a cascade failure within their systems, and before they could contain it, 43 other hubs failed also, cutting off service to vast numbers of telephone customers across the nation. Some say this was an unauthorized date rollover Y2K test. Although that report has not been confirmed, such a test could have resulted in the type of failure reported.

AT&T CEO Michael Armstrong said he believed that a software-generated problem started in two of their frame relay switches and propagated itself to 145 nodes across the frame relay network. AT&T has about 40 percent of the 6,000 network customers in the United States. The outage lasted for 20 hours.

Those customers left without phone service were either hampered or prevented from doing business for what certainly seemed to them an eternity. Banking transfers, manufacturing orders, email services, and many other forms of information systems were affected. As always, those that could least afford the loss — small businesses — were most affected.

Communications Satellites

In May 1998, a communications satellite went down and gave us a preview of coming attractions of what could happen to most, if not all, satellites, including the 24 Global Positioning Navstar Satellites, with the advent of the

Y2K crisis. The *Los Angeles Times* (May 20, 1998) described the fiasco that affected 44 million pager customers in an article entitled "Satellite Problems Cut Service to 90 percent of Pagers":

As many as 90 percent of the more than 44 million pager customers nationwide lost service Tuesday when a communications satellite spun out of control, causing the largest and longest outage of its kind.

The blackout, which hit at 3:18 p.m., affected everyone from doctors and emergency crews to the FBI and other law enforcement agencies to child care providers. It was not immediately clear when service would be restored.

For many, the incident reveals the nation's dependence on high-tech communications and its vulnerabilities. Only the older paging networks — those still using ground-based transmission — were able to maintain service.

Although paging companies have considered backup systems, the costs were seen as prohibitive, given the low probability of such a massive outage.

PageNet, the country's largest paging company with more than 10 million U.S. customers, said that nearly its entire network was inoperable late into the evening.

Millions more customers, served by PageMart, Skytel, MobilComm and Airtouch, as well as phone companies such as MCI and Sprint PCS, also lost service.

"Eighty to 90 percent of everyone out there that has a pager is not getting service right now," said Scott Baradell, a spokesman for Dallas-based PageNet. "This affects virtually every paging company; they all use the same satellite."

The affected satellite, called the Galaxy IV, was built by Hughes Space and Communications in El Segundo and launched five years ago.

The pager problem was of particular concern to doctors. Dr. Steve Dickens, a cardiologist at Cedars-Sinai Medical Center in Los Angeles, said he was spending the night at the hospital because of the problem.

"I have to tell the hospital what to do and how to respond," he said. "Protocol says they can't make a decision without first calling the doctor."

CBS radio and television, the Chinese Television Network and the CNN Airport Network send feeds through Galaxy IV. CBS relies most heavily on Galaxy IV.

The Y2K Impact on the Oil Industry

The world runs on oil. It is drilled for, pumped, refined, and shipped by sophisticated computer-dependent equipment with millions of embedded chips. This is true whether it comes from the Middle East, the North Sea, America, Mexico, or Venezuela. The world cannot survive without oil. *Reuters* reported on October 30, 1997, on the vulnerability of North Sea drilling platforms to the Y2K bug, but this report could apply to any other area of the oil industry as well:

Major oil companies today rang the alarm bell, warning that the so-called millennium computer bug could paralyze the offshore industry in the North Sea — one of the world's biggest oil production areas.

In a worst-case scenario, oil platforms would be forced to shut down just over two years from now simply because automated systems fail to recognize the year 2000, industry experts told a conference here.

Companies such as Royal Dutch/Shell and British Petroleum said they realize they are sitting on a time bomb and are racing against the clock to check millions of microprocessors. But they fear smaller firms have not yet fully grasped the threat to the oil industry.

At the "Project 2000 in Oil and Gas" conference, industry suppliers and service providers were warned that time is running out and urged to act soon to prevent major upheaval. "Stop talking about it, but do it,'" said Ian Smailes, automation project engineer at Total Oil Marine.

The oil industry faces a gargantuan task to fight the millennium bug, illustrated by the fact that a single offshore oil platform may contain over 10,000 microprocessors. Some are deep below sea level, but all need to be checked. To put this into further perspective, there are over 100 platforms in the North Sea alone.

A taste of what might happen if computer systems

fail to recognize a date came from New Zealand last year. There an aluminum smelter ground to a halt for several months because its production system could not deal with a leap year, said David Trim of Shell's year 2000 team.

He told the conference that a worldwide "commercial meltdown" and "economic hardship" were real risks if worst came to worst. "We're talking about something akin to the aftermath of a war," Trim said.

The total costs of getting rid of the millennium bug in Britain have been estimated at 31 billion pounds, while it might be $1.5 trillion for the world as a whole. But Trim said these could be small sums compared with the far bigger investments needed to prop up economies if the problem was not addressed now.

The April 1998 issue of *World Oil* magazine carried an ominous article describing the Y2K situation in the oil industry. It is written by three PhDs with extensive experience in information technology as it is employed in oil production facilities. They made the following assessment:

It is estimated that the average oil and gas firm, starting today, can expect to remediate less than 30 percent of the overall potential failure points in the production environment. This reality shifts the focus of the solution away from trying to fix the problem to planning strategies that would minimize potential damage and mitigate potential safety hazards.

A large drilling company recently ran a test on one of its large ocean-drilling rigs and set the clocks ahead to 2000. The rig immediately shut down, and efforts to get it started again failed. It has also been reported that Shell Oil has found a 20 percent failure rate on their vessels and offshore rigs in their Y2K tests. Systems affected include radar, mapping, ballast monitoring, global maritime distress, and safety equipment. Chevron is also reported to have experienced a high rate of test failures and, as a result, has instituted a new policy to the effect that any ship in port on January 1, 2000, will remain in port, and any ship in transit will remain in transit and carry a minimum of 30 days' provisions on board.

Summary

Business, industry, and, therefore, the world economy is at great risk from the millennium bug — whether banking, securities, insurance, telecommunications, transportation, electric power or other utilities, oil and energy production and distribution, and medicine. Embedded microchips control the lighting, heating, air conditioning, fire and burglar alarms, plumbing, doors, elevators, security systems and assembly lines of hundreds of thousands of businesses, office buildings, malls, airports, etc. Tens of millions of these chips will fail in 2000. No one knows which ones. The bug is the greatest threat to global economies, indeed to modern civilization since the bubonic plague of the Dark Ages (1348–1350) killed one-third of the population of Europe. And it could be the ultimate trigger for a coming global depression.

7

Banking and Financial Systems at Risk

This is not a prediction, it is a certainty — there will be serious disruption in the world's financial services industry. I can't tell whether it's going to be 10 percent business failure, or a meltdown, but it's going to be ugly. It will start with a millennium-induced crash of the world's stock markets 'around the middle of 1999.'

— *The Sunday Times* (August 3, 1997)

I have written extensively over the past year or so about the enormity of the U.S. (and global) debt pyramid ($125 trillion globally with $40 trillion in the U.S., including derivatives); the gigantic U.S. (and global) speculative bubble (epitomized by the highly overpriced U.S. stock market); and the incredible fragility (and vulnerability) of the entire global financial system.

Any number of triggers could implode the present

speculative bubble and bring down the global financial system: massive foreign dumping of U.S. Treasury paper — the "rollover" scenario; a spike in interest rates; a collapse of the dollar; war in the Middle East, accompanied by an Arab oil embargo and Arab-sponsored terrorism on U.S. soil; a political scandal (possible impeachment of the president); or the Asian and Russian financial meltdown.

But the most dangerous of all financial triggers may be the year 2000 millennium bug (coming concurrently with the Asian economic meltdown). Y2K may very possibly trigger a collapse and panic in the global financial and banking system that make all other previous panics in world financial history look like child's play by comparison.

Warnings of an Approaching Bank Crisis

"Before we reach the Year 2000 there is economic loss. Inevitable difficulties are going to emerge. You could end up with a very large problem." — Federal Reserve Chairman Alan Greenspan (*USA Today*, February 26, 1998).

In recent months a number of respected financial authorities have come forward to sound the alarm:

1) On April 4, 1997, the New York Federal Reserve Bank, which sets monetary policy and issues money to the nation's 15,000 banks, issued a "Year 2000 Alert," warning that the Y2K crisis is real and huge, and that if any part of the banking world is not compliant by 2000, that the entire banking system could crash.

2) On May 6, 1997, the Federal Financial Institutions Examination Council (which establishes national S&L and bank reporting standards) issued a year 2000 warning to all U.S. banks and S&Ls that some financial disruptions

would result from the Y2K crisis and, possibly, a world-wide banking failure.

3) On September 8, 1997, the central bank governors of the G-10 (Group of Ten Nations) met in Basel, Switzerland and issued a "Year 2000 Compliance" statement to the world's banks, securities firms, and markets: "It is possible, in the light of the enormous scale and range of financial market participants, that certain applications may fail to operate smoothly on 1st January 2000. It is therefore important that all financial institutions, and in particular market bodies such as exchanges and clearing houses, develop appropriate contingency plans to deal with any interruptions to counterparty trades and payments."

4) On August 3, 1997, *The Sunday Times* of London wrote, "According to the latest research from three of Wall Street's biggest investment banks, the (Y2K) problem could damage New York's financial industry by disabling those banks or brokerage firms that are not prepared for the change. Merrill Lynch, which has a $200 million budget to tackle the problem, says it 'poses a genuine challenge to the networked world.' Morgan Stanley, which is spending $60 million, describes it as "a serious and critical challenge for all modern organizations.: Goldman Sachs says the problem has 'far-reaching implications, not just for the computing services industries but for all businesses.'"

The article entitled "Millennium Bomb May Cripple Wall Street" explained that even if some banks and businesses fix their problems that they will not be able to do business with those who cannot — including those of entire nations and regions. Goldman Sachs was quoted as saying, "The combined computer expertise in all of Europe is not enough to fix that continent's problems in time, even if all those programmers quit their present jobs and worked on nothing but Y2K from now on."

5) In a speech (July 10, 1997) to Congress on the subject of the Y2K threat to the world, Senator Alfonse D'Amato (R-NY) said, "If the work is not completed, the consequences could be devastating for financial institutions, businesses, and consumers . . ."

6) In a *Reuters* report that appeared in the *Netly News*, on October 1, 1997, computer consultant Nick Edwards wrote, "The millennium bug computer crisis threatens a global liquidity lock-up that could send the world's financial markets crashing." Edwards quoted Robert Lau, managing consultant at PA Consulting in Hong Kong, who stated, "It is our prediction that it will only take 5 to 10 percent of the world's bank payments' systems to not work on that one day to create a global liquidity lock-up . . . I don't think the markets have quite grasped the implications of what will happen if the entire system goes down."

How Vulnerable Is the U.S. Banking System to the Millennium Bug?

As of mid-1998, not one major money center bank anywhere claimed to be Y2K compliant. Chase Manhattan and Citicorp (which are typical of large money center banks) must correct 200 million and 400 million lines of code respectively. They will spend about $250 million and $500 million, respectively, on the repairs. Large banks are working harder, faster, and spending more money on Y2K repair to become compliant than smaller banks, but the larger banks have far more lines of code to repair.

As of November 5, 1997, the Comptroller of the Currency told the House Banking Committee that U.S. banks are not doing enough to fix their Y2K computer problems. He warned that a third of community banks are either unaware of the problem or have just started dealing with it.

The Federal Reserve System itself, including its bank wire-transfer system, has 90 million lines of code to inspect, and they are far from being compliant as of this writing. The Fed has less than 175 full-time programmers working on the project, and 500 part-timers.

Y2K Preparations in the Banking Industry

U.S. banks are scrambling to become Y2K compliant. Chairman Greenspan, the Federal Reserve, and the bank regulators are very worried about the banking system and are putting extreme pressure on the banks to become Y2K compliant. This probably gives the banking system a huge advantage over other industries that have no such pressure.

Greenspan participated in a congressional question-and-answer session with Senator Bennett's Y2K committee. He was very candid in admitting that the Federal Reserve was prepared to lend tens of billions of dollars if the bank computers break down and the banks can't meet the demand for cash. He also made it very clear that all banks are not going to be prepared when he stated, "Inevitable difficulties are going to emerge . . . You could end up with a very large problem."

In the *Year 2000 Survival Newsletter*, Jim Lord wrote about the banks and the Y2K crisis:

There has been some good news and some bad from the banking industry, and the two more or less balance each other out.

The good news is the banking industry is getting set up for some industry-wide Y2K testing activities for the FedWire, Automated Clearing House (ACH), and Mortgage Payment systems. These will be beneficial because they might give the banks, as well as the public, some indication of the actual status of the industry (if the press is allowed access to any of the testing results, that is).

Also good news is some of the reports coming from people who work for banks that Y2K is a top priority issue because the federal banking regulators are really starting to hold their feet to the fire.

There was also a fair share of bad news. Internal surveys indicate banks are making very slow progress. One, conducted in February 1998, showed, for example, that 60 percent of the banks surveyed were still in the assessment phase, 36 percent were fixing flawed computer code and only 4 percent were conducting testing. None of the banks was completed.

In summary, 96 percent of the banks surveyed were less than 50 percent completed with their repair process. Several months of these internal banking surveys can be found on the Internet at www.market-partners.com.

The Federal Reserve Bank is Stockpiling Billions for Y2K Preparation

On July 29, 1998, a regional banker in New England stated that the Federal Reserve System is stockpiling currency in preparation for Y2K-generated bank runs in 1999. A Fed spokesman did confirm that the Federal Reserve will make liquidity available.

However, as the *Boston Business Journal* (July 27, 1998) wrote,

> . . . Most worrisome, though, bankers, say, is what they cannot control.

> One South Shore banker says his bank is convinced that Social Security, disability and other federal entitlement payments will be bogged down by Year 2000-crippled computer systems, and he is preparing to pay his bank's depositors based on previous pay stubs, then work with the government to be repaid once the computer system is repaired.

> And, like North Shore Bank's McCormack, who is already making plans for extra bank security, McManus says BankBoston is scheduling back-up generators in case electrical power is interrupted in the days and weeks following the turn of the century.

> Such scenarios could lead fearful depositors to stockpile currency in the months leading up to 2000, perhaps severely straining the currency system, according to a Boston economist.

> "For the first time in many years, the Federal

Reserve System and other government agencies are worried about widespread runs on the banks," says State Street Bank & Trust Company chief economist Fred Breimyer. "The Federal Reserve and Treasury Department are very much aware this could happen, and they are making provisions for a substantial oversupply of currency to meet the currency drain," he says.

Breimyer says the Treasury Department is now printing extra currency, especially in large denominations such as $100 bills, in preparation for expected depositor demand for cash. Officials at the Federal Reserve Bank of Boston say the central bank is preparing for potential heightened demand for cash, but declined to elaborate on the specifics of their plans. "We certainly expect to meet cash demand during that time," says Federal Reserve Bank spokesman Tom Lavelle. "We already have a substantial inventory on hand as a matter of course," he says.

Still, banking industry officials concede that all efforts here to prepare U.S. banking systems for the next millennium may not be enough. They say that the worst threat could come from overseas, where Asian and European financial institutions lag far behind their American counterparts in making the Year 2000 fix, says Shepard Remis, a Boston attorney who has examined the Year 2000 computer problem and its potential impact on banks and businesses.

Banks Are at Risk from Their Customers' and Loan Losses

Fixing a bank's own computers is both time consuming and costly, but at least it is manageable. But what about the computers of the banks' major commercial customers, and the bank loans outstanding to those customers? Banks are having a very hard time assessing the Y2K readiness (and, therefore, the credit risk) of their customers. The problem is that banks don't have the trained staff needed to evaluate their customers' Y2K readiness. This is a very serious problem because if they can't determine how safe their commercial borrowers are, they will have to severely clamp down on credit and raise interest rates. A credit crunch in the midst of the unfolding Y2K crisis will not be helpful.

On March 18, 1998, the *Wall Street Journal* carried an article entitled "Banks Could See a Rise In Loan Losses Due to Year 2000 Computer Glitches" that reported the following warning: "Problem loans may well rise if some borrowers fail to upgrade their computers in time . . . Banks considered most vulnerable by analysts include those lending primarily to small businesses . . . Also at risk are banks with significant overseas exposure."

A Barclays Bank Executive Fears a Global Crash in 2000

The Sunday Times of London (March 29, 1998) quoted an anonymous executive at Barclays Bank, one of England's largest, oldest, and most prestigious banks, who gave an interesting (off-the-record) insider's view of what is coming:

A senior executive at Barclays has warned people

to sell their homes, stockpile their cash and buy gold in case of a global economic collapse caused by the millennium computer bug. This extraordinary warning is echoed by other bank managers who fear a run on deposits.

When computers click over from the year 99 to 00 experts say many applications will crash and create indecipherable data. Under this "doomsday scenario" global markets and economies may fail to cope with millions of computers crashing at once. It is feared currencies and stock exchanges could go into free fall, slashing the value of savings.

The Y2K scenario is now being treated seriously because European banks are struggling to change systems in time for the single currency. Many have not even begun to tackle the millennium bug. From next year, insurance policies, bank accounts and other financial products must incorporate the year 2000 in many of next year's transactions.

Experts are unsure how computers will cope: they may produce huge bills and interest calculations, shut down completely, or carry on as usual.

"The average man or woman does not appreciate what is going to happen," said the Barclays executive, who wishes to remain anonymous. "I'm going to plan for the absolute worst — I am talking about the need to start buying candles, tinned food and bottled water from mid-1999 onwards. People think that I am mad, but a company director I met last week is intending to set up a commune and buy a shotgun because the potential for looting is also quite high."

Although many may see this view as far-fetched, a senior Midland executive was also pessimistic: "Gold wouldn't be a bad thing to get into. But I would wait and see if that would be the most secure thing."

This quotation is not from some Y2K fanatic or gloom-and-doomer. It is from a top executive at one of the world's largest and most prestigious banks in a large, respected London newspaper. The same article went on to point out that "such is the lack of confidence, that London Electric is planning to issue its engineers bicycles in case traffic lights are not working." It seems that there are executives in England who are taking Y2K seriously.

U.S. and Global Banks Are Interdependent and Therefore Vulnerable

The U.S. banking system is highly interdependent and interconnected. If 80 percent of the banks become compliant, and 20 percent don't, the 20 percent can bring down the 80 percent. If 95 percent are compliant, and 5 percent are noncompliant, the 5 percent can bring down the 95 percent. It is axiomatic that bad data corrupt good data. That's why Alan Greenspan has insisted that there must be 100 percent Y2K compliance in the U.S. banking system.

The entire global financial system is intertwined like a giant spider web — the stock markets, bond markets, derivatives markets (totaling $82 trillion), commodities markets, the banking system, governments (which issue and trade in debt), and telecommunications. This gigantic global financial network is all tied together by computers, many of which are noncompliant. If or when the Asian computers falter, they can take down the Wall Street or London computers. If any of these systems go, they can take down all the rest like a giant power blackout that rapidly spreads until the whole countryside is darkened. This is called "systemic risk."

Recently David Iacino, senior manager of the Millennium Project at the nation's 15th largest bank, Bank-Boston, which has $65 billion in assets and 760 branches and offices in 24 countries, testified before Congress regarding the interdependence of the global banking system:

> The Year 2000 computer problem is pervasive and is global in scope. It affects not only the financial services industry, but all industries. Each business is itself both a customer and a supplier in the food chain of international commerce . . .

> Financial institutions are extremely dependent on one another as well as common service providers for the interchange of electronic commerce . . . The increasing globalization of the business enterprise radiates these dependencies beyond our borders to include financial institutions worldwide . . . There are significant risks associated with such tightly woven interdependencies . . .

> The majority of the critical work, however, lies ahead . . . There is an enormous interdependency among all financial institutions on the viability of the payments system . . . All common financial services providers must be prepared. All systems

and application vendors must be prepared. All suppliers and customers must be prepared. And then we must all test the interdependencies we share well before the year 2000 to ensure stability of the system not only domestically, but also globally.

What if your local bank's computer is fixed, but it is unable to communicate with 5,000 to 10,000 other noncompliant banks (i.e., the "lock-out" scenario) around the world? How will your bank cash checks or clear credit cards issued by noncompliant banks? How will other banks cash your checks and credit card purchases? All banks are at risk. Therefore, all bank customers are at risk.

Banks rely heavily on third-party transaction processing, outsourced services, and system interoperability within their operations. A complex web of business and system relationships has been constructed through incremental changes and customizations incorporated over many years. The banking system is far more complex and vulnerable than any one bank's computer. No bank, or bank computer, is an island unto itself.

Although U.S. banks have completed 30 percent of their compliance efforts, according to surveys conducted by Gartner Group, Inc., "They have a probability of 10 percent system failure," says Lou Marcoccio, director of year 2000 research at the Gartner Group.

The Status of Overseas Banks and the Risk to Global Trade

Eighty percent of all computer code exists in nations outside the United States. The banking system is international. There's no place to hide. Europe's banks are far behind America's and are preoccupied with programming for their new European currency — the Euro — in 1999. They will not be compliant. The rest of the world is far behind Europe. Asian banks have done little or nothing; Latin American banks are just now hearing about the problem. Russia, China, and Africa have barely begun to look at the problem. They will not be compliant by 2000.

In December 1997, William Rybock, associate director for banking supervision, said that the Fed is considering plans to ban the import of computerized data from any noncompliant foreign bank in 2000. Rybock said that the Fed is working on contingency plans in case banks in Latin America or other areas of the world don't get their systems fixed. He said the United States might ban transactions between U.S. banks and noncompliant foreign banks. The Fed is preparing for a collapse of the international banking system and international trade.

The timing of the Y2K crisis is very problematic internationally. Much of the world (especially Asia) is moving into severe recession or deflation (toward depression). The Asian meltdown, now accelerating in Japan and South Korea, will greatly hinder a Y2K fix in those countries. The timing of the European currencies conversion to the Euro in 1999 is almost totally distracting Europe from fixing their Y2K problems. Most experts agree that any large organization needs a minimum of two and a half years to repair their Y2K code. However, Europe will only begin serious Y2K efforts in January 1999.

To make matters worse, a global trend toward deflation now is about to be greatly exacerbated by the Y2K crisis.

Japan Is the Biggest Banking Domino of All

The *Australian Financial Review* (October 30, 1997) carried the following warning about Japan:

The major economy most vulnerable to an acute financial crisis is now Japan, according to a world authority on international finance. Morris Goldstein, of the Institute for International Economics in Washington D.C., said yesterday that problems with financial systems were "fairly widespread" among the major economies of North Asia — Japan, South Korea, and China.

"But if you look at where systemic risk is largest, it's in Japan — there's no doubt about it, because it comes on top of other things that have happened there," he said in an interview in Sydney . . . He added that Japan was set for "a truly world-class banking crisis." Already three Japanese banks had collapsed.

A senior economist with Nomura Securities in Tokyo, Nobuya Nemoto, agrees that the crisis could soon enter an acute phase. "Another two or three banks will collapse this fiscal year, to the end of next March, and the Deposit Insurance Corporation is supposed to support them, but they have no funds left," he said. "The problem has become so big that it is politically impossible to use public funds to rescue them."

Banking Panic:
Will the Y2K Crisis Precipitate Bank Runs in 1999?

"Since a significant number of people are planning for money and investment retrieval just prior to the millennium (2000), a panic could easily occur regarding savings, mutual funds, stocks, etc. Any news publicizing this issue just before 2000, could easily add to the panic. Banks and financial institutions in other countries will see critical failures, and this will also gain news attention." — A representative of the Gartner Group testifying before the House Banking Committee on November 4, 1997.

As the general public becomes more knowledgeable about the Y2K crisis, their nervousness about the banking system and the stock market is likely to grow. In September/October 1997, the Gartner Group interviewed 1,100 computer industry executives worldwide, and 38 percent said they might withdraw their personal assets from the banks and investment companies before December 31, 1999.

For every $100 you think you have in your bank checking account, your bank has just $3 or so of actual cash in its vault. The rest exists in the bank's computers, as loans. At some point, probably in mid-1999, people who understand the Y2K crisis may start pulling their money out of the banks. As Gary North recently wrote:

Your bank has only a little cash in it. Whatever you've deposited has been loaned out. You have been promised that you can draw out all of your money at any time. The banker assumes that you won't do this, and if you do, some other depositor will put in about as much money.

Sometime between now and June 2000 — probably in July 1999 — this assumption will die, all over the world. When depositors see that their money may disappear in the scrambling of the banks' computers, they will go down and demand payment in cash. On that day, the mother of all bank runs will begin. It will spread to every bank on earth.

The run may not start in the United States. It could well start in Japan. Japanese housewives control the pool of investment money in Japan. If they think their families' capital is at risk, they will very politely go down and get cash. Japanese banks use U.S.-built mainframe computers with the millennium bug built in.

What can the world's central banks do to stem the panic? First, they can get their governments to limit cash withdrawals by law. Then they can print paper money. If they do either or both, this will end men's faith in the banking system and the capital markets based on it. Capital markets will collapse in a wave of selling, while consumer goods prices denominated in paper money will soar.

We will see a breakdown in money payments. The social division of labor will collapse as a result. Unemployment will soar to levels never seen in the Great Depression. Computer-denominated wealth will disappear.

All modern governments rest on banks. Without the banks, tax collection stops. The national tax collectors cannot come and take a percentage of your garden. Governments will not be able to pay money out or take money in. Banks are the heart of the tax and payments system, and fractional reserve banking as a system will not survive the year 2000. (To subscribe to Gary North's excellent newsletter, *Remnant Review*, write to: Remnant Review, 1217 St. Paul Street, Baltimore, MD 21202; 410-234-0691; $129/year.)

The Securities Industry

The U.S. stock market came within an hour of a total meltdown on October 19–20, 1987, and again on October 27–28, 1997. It was not just the stock prices (which dropped 507 and 554 points respectively) that came close to melting down. There was a chain reaction of paperwork logjams, computer malfunctions, jammed phone switchboards, 800 numbers in gridlock, etc. This near meltdown on Wall Street was primarily due to a sudden overwhelming volume of orders — first sell orders, then buy orders. Trading systems went into gridlock.

The volume of shares now traded on a given day can range from 500 million to a billion, with forecasts of 3 to 5 billion share days in the next year or two. On October 28, 1997 ("Happy Tuesday," which followed "Black Monday"), trading volume was 1.2 billion shares. All of this trading and the massive bookkeeping that follows is done by computers, both for individual stocks and mutual funds.

As in the banking industry, Wall Street is now 100 percent dependent on computers, and this vast array of computers is not Y2K compliant. Australia's *Financial Review* estimates that the total price tag for the U.S. securities industry's "Y2K fix" will exceed $5 billion. Merrill Lynch alone will spend over $200 million. But, as with the banks, each element of the system is interdependent on another element. Noncompliant computers or corrupted data can bring down compliant computers and infect clean data. And the securities industry computers are totally tied into the banking industry computers, which if not 100 percent compliant, can infect the former.

On November 1, 1997, Market Partners, Inc., a company that sells Y2K services to banks, published the following scenario for a computer meltdown on Wall Street:

> Take the following scenario — a securities trade transaction. A trade will involve many firms over the course of three days to complete processing. Information must pass between these third-party organizations and proprietary systems before the trade is successful. In processing the trade, data will be sent and received between various entities, involving the customer, the administrator, the trading desk, brokerage providers, utility providers (DTC, NSCC, and other interested parties), clearing banks, custodian banks, beneficiaries, and exchanges.

> Critical calculations are derived based upon timing of the transaction, including the calculation of interest, generating margins, applying valuations, commissions, settlement, clearing of funds, and disbursement. The Year 2000 related risks created from this scenario have significant business ramifications. A single point of failure could generate a chain reaction which could cause huge operational implications within the institution, resulting in

failed trades, incorrect posting, manual intervention, unfulfilled contracts, angry customers, and
lack of confidence for the institution by its share-
holders.

What if one system fails in the chain of systems that
process the trade? What if nobody fails, but the
data is incorrect when the trade has completed?
How do the risks associated with cross-company
failures get mitigated, or at least diminished to a
narrow scope with minimal impact and recovery?
Even with legal remedies, the financial institution
may be jeopardized.

What will be the impact of a major "Y2K fix" on earn-
ings for major U.S. corporations? How will they fare if
they don't get it fixed? At what point will investors begin
to panic and flee from the most overpriced stock market
and mutual funds in history? Today, most investors have
a very limited knowledge of the Y2K problem — its scope
and magnitude. That will change dramatically over the
next year, as the mainline media finally jump on the story.
At some point, public optimism, euphoria, complacency,
and apathy will turn to panic and the greatest of all stock-
market crash in history will ensue in America, and possibly be followed by a deflationary depression of epic proportions.

Security Industry Preparedness

If the stock market comes tumbling down, everything else
in the economy and financial system will come crashing
down not far behind it. This is why Greenspan, the Fed,
President Clinton, and Wall Street are working so hard to
defy gravity and keep the stock market propped up. They

have to continue the hype to keep the middle class pouring their savings and retirements funds into the market (or mutual funds) so that the insiders have someone to sell their shares to.

Wall Street runs on computers and on confidence. Its computers almost went into gridlock during the crash of October 1987 and again during the crash of October 1997 — maxed out by the highest volumes of panic selling in U.S. stock market history. In 1987, the stock market in Brussels, Belgium was shut down for two hours because of Y2K-related problems with futures software. In those two hours, lost commissions totaled $1 million, but the problem was relatively minor and easily fixed. Adrian Peracchio, board member of *Newsday*, says there have already been more than 10,000 similar, "minor" Y2K glitches that have happened in America over the past year.

On July 13, 1998, the securities industry on Wall Street ran a relatively minor test of simulated tracking in mortgage-backed securities and declared in high-profile, glowing headlines that "Wall Street's Y2K Test Goes Very Well," "Wall Street Passes Y2K Glitch Without a Hitch," "Wall Street is Okay!" A series of such tests will be conducted through March 1999. However, this test excluded international trades, and was limited to less than 1 percent of the normal daily volume.

It is unlikely that these minor, simulated tests can prove anything about the viability of the securities industry's computers during billion-share days when there is panic selling and problems in hundreds of other systems — from banking to derivatives, from commodities to options, from telecommunications to electric power industries, from foreign banks to foreign securities markets. All of these systems interface with Wall Street every day and many of them are likely to be having problems after January 1, 2000.

These Y2K tests are conducted primarily for public relations — to instill public confidence that the stock market trading systems will be fine and that the public can keep buying stocks, bonds, and mutual funds ad infinitum. Without that confidence, the stock market will fall.

The recent and future Wall Street tests also serve another purpose. They will help protect the big firms from the massive lawsuits that are going to result from the Y2K crisis. Their argument will be, "We tested, we did everything possible, and the system still pulled us down."

What Can Go Wrong in the Securities Industry?

The following illustration of what can go wrong when the computers malfunction on Wall Street was broadcast on CNN on June 5, 1997, about Smith Barney, the well-known stock brokerage and investment banking firm:

> A computer glitch at Smith Barney overnight briefly put $19 million into each of hundreds of thousands of customer accounts, the brokerage said Thursday morning. . . . Smith Barney spokesman Gordon Andrew said customers were not affected in any way. At some point overnight, he said, roughly $19 million appeared in separate entries for each Smith Barney financial management account. The brokerage has 525,000 such accounts.

Jim Lord, writing in his *Year 2000 Survival Newsletter*, had this observation about this $10 trillion computer glitch on Wall Street:

Now, as Paul Harvey would say, "Here's the rest of the story." The computer programmers who fouled this one up were attempting to make Y2K repairs to a database. The changes had been successfully tested off-line, so the crew decided to conduct a live test in conjunction with the firm's main software. The result of the test was an accidental deposit of $19,000,000 into each account. The total error exceeded ten trillion dollars.

Now, what does this incident reveal about the year 2000 problem in general and the Y2K susceptibility of the banking and stock brokerage industries in particular? Consider the general aspect first.

Fixing the year 2000 problem in computers is the easy part. Finding the code that needs to be fixed is significantly harder. Testing the repairs afterwards is, by far, the hardest part of all. That's why testing typically takes half or more of all the time and money used in the whole repair process.

Using repaired computer code before it has been stringently tested (as happened in this instance) is highly dangerous and has the potential to produce horrifying side effects. As we move into 1998 and especially in 1999, more and more software will be undergoing Y2K repair and testing. Most enterprises today are trying to fix their software by the end of 1998 so they can use 1999 for testing. Accordingly, the incidence of computer accidents will increase dramatically in 1998 and 1999.

Smith Barney was very fortunate. They had a big problem, but they were able to recognize the problem immediately. If this problem had occurred in a way that was invisible, there's no telling what the consequences might have been.

Smith Barney was also lucky in another way. They were able to contain the problem in their own computers. The banking and investment industries are the most intensely interconnected elements of the global economy. If, because of invisibility, this error had managed to leak (or burst) outside the confines of the Smith Barney computers before being detected, the results could have been catastrophic. And not just for them. We may have all been lucky on June 5th.

This story is rich in instructive value because it so dramatically demonstrates the fragility of the world's banking and investment systems. The foundation of our banking system's stability is public confidence. Even a slight erosion in that confidence could collapse that foundation. When you build your castle on the sand, it doesn't take a tidal wave to knock it down. A garden hose can do the job. Efforts to fix the year 2000 problem will almost certainly cause accidents that will erode that confidence.

The year 2000 problem is a monumental threat to the global banking and investment systems. You should have no more money therein than you can afford to (a) lose or (b) be able to live without for an extended period.

Will There Be a Meltdown in the $82 Trillion Global Financial Derivatives Market?

The most speculative financial bubble in the world is 100 percent computerized. What will the Y2K crisis do to this highly leveraged, super-speculative global debt pyramid? In the past I have analyzed derivatives, and their risk to the entire world financial system. Wall Street is ingenious in creating new, highly leveraged speculative paper schemes for separating investors from their money and ringing the cash registers for Wall Street (i.e., REITS, options, junk bonds, leveraged buyouts, securitizing of debts, etc.).

Wall Street has created dozens of extremely complicated, highly leveraged gimmicks called derivatives contracts, which threaten to sink the U.S. (and global) financial system. This gargantuan financial Frankenstein monster has quickly grown to a $52 trillion highly leveraged computer/paper pyramid in the United States alone, and to $82 trillion worldwide.

Derivatives are artificial financial instruments that derive their value from actual underlying investments such as stocks, bonds, and real estate. They include interest rate swaps, interest rate options, swaptions, caps, floors, collars, collateralized mortgage obligations, commodity futures and options, forward commodity contracts, equity-linked bank deposits, IOs (interest-only mortgages), POs (principal-only mortgages), synthetic securities, MITTS (Market Index Targeted Term Securities), Eurodollar futures, yield curve notes, etc.

These computer-generated investments can carry as much as 100 to 1 leverage (a 1 percent rise in value leads to a 100 percent gain in equity invested; and a 1 percent decline wipes out your entire equity). Long U.S. government bonds declined 29 percent in 1994. Imagine having bought those with 100 to 1 leverage.

Time magazine (April 11, 1994) described derivatives collectively as "computer-generated, hyper-sophisticated financial instruments that use the public's massive bet on securities to create a parallel universe of side bets and speculative mutations so vast that the underlying $20 trillion involved is almost five times the total value of all stocks traded on the NYSE in a month and three times the size of the nation's GDP."

It should be remembered that the $1 trillion stock market crash in 1987 was precipitated in the derivatives market.

Derivatives, in theory, were originally created to reduce market risk through various hedging techniques. But, in reality, recent massive derivatives contracts have introduced more risk because of the incredible volume of money that rides on them. These "side bets" pull with them a real world of securities worth 30 times their value.

Time says, "These breakneck derivative deals are possible because Wall Street today has transformed itself into a virtually seamless network of computer-linked brokers, dealers, and exchanges around the globe. The trades take place in an electronic neverland that can be entered from anywhere in the world.

"Billion-dollar transactions involving derivatives or other securities that once took hours or days to handle are now routinely completed in seconds — with all the potential risk or reward that comes with instant gains and losses." And so, Wall Street's speculative bubble continues to grow as big banks and brokerage firms scramble to create ever-more exotic derivatives products.

Our major U.S. banks and securities firms have been the key players in the global derivatives market. If Y2K triggers a financial collapse, and it probably will, this derivatives' bubble will come crashing down and may well take down some of America's largest multinational banks and investment brokers.

Trillions of Dollars at Risk Due to Derivatives Trades

As *Time* (May 25, 1998) wrote,

> J. P. Morgan, America's fifth largest bank, got bad news this year when several South Korean firms suddenly repudiated their derivative contracts, leaving Morgan out some $500 million. America's biggest lender, Chase Manhattan, saw its "non-performing" assets in Asia triple in the first three months of 1998, to $243 million, due in part to derivatives. At the end of last year, its total risk from Asian derivatives — should others default — was more than $3 billion. Bankers Trust's derivatives' delinquencies have leaped from zero to $330 million in a year and the compass points to Indonesian and Thai clients. In total, the bank has some $5 billion of derivative credit exposure in Asia . . .
>
> And now comes the bad news. Some $10 trillion (yes, $10,000,000,000,000) in derivative contracts are set to mature this year for U.S. bankers, and the U.S. bankers are holding their collective breath to see which of their Asian clients will pay up. Many won't. "Those who believe there won't be any further derivative losses from Asia couldn't be more

mistaken," says Edward Furash, a bank consultant based in Washington.

The institution holding the biggest bag of derivatives is Chase, with $7.6 trillion. Interestingly, Chase raised the red flag in its 1997 annual report, noting, "Management expects there will be an increase in nonperforming assets in 1998 primarily as a result of the deterioration of credit conditions in a number of Asian countries." Unlike other banks, Chase refused to talk publicly about its derivatives exposure with clients that are below investment grade, but it already has more than $1 billion in total nonperforming assets. A report issued by the OCC examiners puts its total credit risks from derivatives at $81.9 billion, four times stockholders' equity.

As Gary North commented in *Remnant Review* (June 5, 1998):

Think about this. Chase Manhattan Bank (the Rockefeller bank) has money tied up in electronic promises to pay — derivatives — equal to the entire production of the U.S. economy in 1998. Banks will fail before 2000. They may begin to fail even before the Y2K panic hits. But surely when the Y2K panic hits in 1999, it will bring down debt-ridden banks. Paper promises will die.

The derivatives market is a gigantic disaster waiting to happen. The free market has created these derivatives with the help of government guarantees for banking. But this is basically a free-market endeavor, as surely as the modern computer is a free-market invention. When the economy crashes, electronic promises to pay will collapse.

As the *Wall Street Journal* in its March 18, 1998 article (quoted above about Y2K-related loan risk exposure) said, "... also at risk are banks with significant overseas exposure." The large U.S. money center banks have trillions of dollars in overseas loan exposure via derivatives. Does that seem significant to you?

8

The Electric Power Grid Is at Risk Due to Y2K

Today we are focusing on the effect of the computer glitches on perhaps the most fundamental necessity of our modern society: electrical energy. Energy provided by our electrical utilities is a critical catalyst to operation of virtually every sector of our nation's economy. If power shuts down, the rest of our society will shut down in its wake. The year 2000 problem has the potential to short-circuit our nation's power sources and severely disrupt the delivery of energy to the American public through systematic power failures.

— Congresswoman Constance Morella
in congressional testimony on May 14, 1998

Let's stop pretending Y2K isn't a major threat to our way of life. There's too much at stake for such

uninformed wishful thinking. I say we must act as
if we were preparing for war.
— Edward Yardeni in a speech to the Bank for
International Settlements on April 7, 1998

There is a virtual certainty that we'll have brownouts and some regional blackouts . . . I think the
chances . . . throughout the grid are about 80 percent.
— Senator Robert Bennett, chairman of the Senate
committee on the Y2K problem on June 12, 1998

Electric power is the Achilles heel of western civilization
in the coming Y2K computer crisis. According to the Electric Power Research Institute, the electric power industry
in America is totally dependent upon computers and computer chips. In the 1970s and 1980s, all mechanical
switches were pulled out of electric power utilities and
replaced with electronic switches run from main computers.

As Edward and Jennifer Yourdon wrote in their excellent book, *Time Bomb 2000: What the Year 2000 Crisis Means
to You*:

> With little doubt, electric power is one of the funda-
> mental linchpins of modern society. If power shuts
> down, a great deal of the rest of society shuts down
> with it. The nation's electrical generating system is
> definitely an area where ripple effect problems
> could occur.

> Within the U.S. there are 6,000 electrical generating
> units, 500,000 miles of bulk transmission lines,
> 12,000 major substations, and vast numbers of

lower-voltage transformers. They're all linked together on a grid by computer mainframes, and
even with redundancy and fail-safe mechanisms, it
is still possible for a problem in one section of the
system to ripple elsewhere.

There could be year 2000 bugs in the computer
software associated with the electrical power grid.
Each of the 6,000 generating units throughout the
U.S. has its own computer system to regulate the
amount of electricity that is generated by hydroelectric dams, oil-burning generators, or nuclear
generators.

The entire network, or grid, is controlled regionally
by more than 100 separate control centers that coordinate responsibilities jointly for the impact upon
real time network operations throughout the country. The control centers have computer systems,
too, and these, too, can fail. These systems do have
date calculations embedded within them; as such,
they are vulnerable to year 2000 failures."

In addition to many millions of lines of noncompliant
codes in electric power plants' mainframe computers,
each plant can have up to 10,000 embedded chips. They
are everywhere in the old systems, and the industry has a
lot of old systems (computers and software), based on
languages, packages, and processors that require skills
that are gradually being lost as new technology is developed.

Most of these chips cannot easily be replaced. Many
chips are buried so deep in mechanical hardware that they
cannot even be located without tearing down factory

machinery or even entire buildings. Fixing the year 2000 problem in this industry is more complicated than for banking or administrative applications. The systems are more difficult to audit because some are so old that documentation about them has been lost.

Real-time systems, which can be very complex, are used to control or monitor very high-value computer processors. Typically, a power station will have scores of real-time systems. For a power station, the cost of an unexpected shutdown can be hundreds of thousands of dollars. Therefore, the pressure to keep the production process running is great. As a result, production managers resist changes to embedded systems.

Hence, most of these systems have never been upgraded. To fix the Y2K problems in electric power utilities will take tens of thousands of people who understand embedded-systems technology, the production processes, and the commercial impact of mistakes in a manufacturing environment. Such people are rare.

The Electric Power Grid Domino Effect

Imagine this scenario: At 00:00:03 on the morning of January 1, 2000, approximately 20–25 percent of the online utility plants on the North American continent trip and go off-line; approximately 20–30 percent of the protective switch gears fail to operate correctly, leading to the loss of another 20 percent of the online power generation. A rolling blackout travels across America as many cities are plunged into darkness.

Is such a scenario far-fetched? No, in fact we have already had serious power failures, brownouts, or blackouts in recent years, even without the Y2K crisis. Most were temporary failures and were weather-related — due to tornadoes, blizzards, hurricanes, floods, or extreme heat or cold waves. In 1965, chaos ensued when much of the Northeast was shut down by a blackout. In the summer of 1977, there was a power blackout that plunged New York into darkness for days. On July 3, 1996, a power outage knocked out electricity in parts of eight western states and two Canadian provinces. In the winter of 1998, there was a historic power outage in eastern Canada and the northeast United States that left millions of homes and businesses without power for over 30 days. In early 1998, there was a power-grid failure in Auckland, New Zealand that shut down all electric power to businesses and homes in the affected area for four months. Almost 25 percent of the businesses in that area were bankrupted due to the power blackout.

Twenty-two percent of U.S. electric power comes from 109 nuclear power plants. This nuclear-generated electricity is as reliable and safe as the computers running those plants. There are currently 110 commercial nuclear power reactors licensed to operate in 32 states. Six states (Connecticut, New Jersey, Maine, Vermont, South Carolina, and Illinois) rely on nuclear power for more than 50 percent of their electricity. Thirteen additional states rely on nuclear power for 25–50 percent of their electricity. Three of the six major regions of the country depend on nuclear power for at least 25 percent of their electricity.

However, if these nuclear plants are not Y2K compliant by December 31, 1999 (and they probably won't be), the Nuclear Regulatory Commission (not wanting to risk core meltdown — a Chernobyl or Three Mile Island accident) will shut them down. A 22 percent drop in electric power generation (40–100 percent in some states) will affect major areas in the power grid that don't rely on nuclear power. Even if your local power plant is Y2K compliant, it could be shorted out by an overload in the power grid and take down your local system. In Ontario, Canada, over 60 percent of the power depends on nuclear plants.

On December 24, 1996, a document entitled "Information Notice 96–70: Year 2000 Effect on Computer System Software" was issued by the Nuclear Regulatory Commission. It contained several ominous paragraphs that indicate that the regulators do not understand the depth of risk for nuclear power plants from Y2K: "The Year 2000 issue affects everyone. It will have an impact on state and local governments, NRC licensees, and businesses. The magnitude of the Year 2000 issue poses a challenge to all those potentially affected. Dates are involved in many facets of computer systems and software. Neither industry nor the federal government has yet identified the scope of the situation."

It then warns about specific problem areas. These, too, are not reassuring: "This issue may affect NRC licensees in many different ways. For example, computer software used to calculate radioactive doses, or to account for radioactive decay may not recognize the turn of the century, which could lead to incorrectly calculated doses or exposure times for treatment planning. Other examples of software that may be affected include security control, radiation monitoring, technical specification surveillance testing, and accumulated burn-up programs."

Another domino in U.S. power generation is the delivery of coal and fuel oil to U.S. power stations at a time when computer-dependent railroads, ocean shipping, pipelines and other delivery systems may also be in gridlock due to the Y2K meltdown.

Major urban power generation stations rely on coal for as much as 20–25 percent of their fuel requirements. How can the power plants get delivery of coal if the railroad system goes down due to noncompliance? Most power plants that rely on coal or fuel oil have only one to three weeks of fuel storage. After that, if the trains don't deliver, the lights go out. Rail-car movement and inventory is now tracked by date-sensitive computer programs. Rail switching is no longer done manually, but is controlled by date-sensitive computers (in many instances, antiquated) and embedded controls.

Will America's Electric Power Utilities Be Y2K Compliant?

In early 1997, Lexibridge Corporation of Shelton, Connecticut, surveyed 12 public utilities (gas, electricity, water) and found that 55 percent had a Y2K repair plan. They might not have started working on the problem yet, but at least 55 percent had a plan on paper. Of the remaining 45 percent, 9 percent of these utilities planned at least to think about Y2K in 1997, but 36 percent replied that they had no plan to even consider repairing Y2K.

Olsten Corporation of Melville, New York, conducted a similar survey with a larger sample size. Their results showed that only 68 percent of responding utilities had even considered formulating a Y2K repair plan. Of the few utilities that have actually formulated plans and begun work, 37 percent report being way behind schedule, according to industry expert Capers Jones.

Similar situations are faced all over the world. In August 1997, the British Government's Health and Safety Executive commissioned the Glasgow-based group, Real Time Engineering, to study the risks that embedded chips pose to a sampling of public utility companies. The September 25, 1997 issue of *Computer Weekly News* reports that 20 percent of all business-critical computer systems in British oil, petrochemical, power, and aviation manufacturing firms are susceptible. This doesn't mean that one in five companies are noncompliant; this means that one in five computerized systems in every company is noncompliant. Gerry Docherty, who manages Real Time Engineering, stated that there was "no hope" for many of the companies they tested; they would catastrophically and permanently fail, and their customers would just have to do without life-sustaining services after 2000.

The June 2, 1997, *Newsweek* article entitled "The Day the World Shuts Down" described that when Hawaiian Electric utility in Honolulu ran tests on its system to see if it would be affected by the Y2K bug, "basically it just stopped working." If the problem had not been addressed, Hawaii would have blacked out on January 1, 2000.

The problem of possible utility shutdowns is exacerbated by the fact that when a local power company goes down, it must draw power from the grid to restart its system. It takes six times normal power for that plant to get started back up again. But what if 20 percent of the national power grid goes down from Y2K-induced failures? Could restarting the downed portion overload the entire power grid and pull down the rest of the system?

Remember, power generation depends upon power generation.

If the entire U.S. power grid were to go down, where would the power come from (requiring six times the normal power) to restart it? This is the ultimate doomsday scenario that the pessimists worry about. Is it likely? Probably not! More likely, we will see rolling, fluctuating brownouts or blackouts for a period of a few weeks or even months. Remember, however, it took four months to restart the power in Central Auckland, New Zealand. However, it is not totally inconceivable to imagine the entire grid going down. If that were to happen, the convulsions across America would be unimaginable.

How much is the U.S. power grid at risk from a Y2K meltdown? Many leaders in the electric or nuclear power industries deny that there is a problem or they take a sanguine "party-line" approach and say that everything is okay; we'll get it fixed. However, other industry insiders (who can only talk anonymously) quite literally are terrified.

Dr. Gary North recently wrote about the potential problems with the U.S. power grid:

> Electrical power is the Big One. This is the heart of western civilization. If the power generation plants fail because of the effects of the millennium bug, it's literally over for the West. We are all hooked up to the system. But no public utility will survive if the power goes down and stays down. No business will survive. It will be a total breakdown. As Roberto Vacca titled his 1973 book, it would mean *The Coming Dark Age.*

Deep concern is presently being voiced about potential Y2K power failures in Britain, where contingency plans are being set up in case of a nationwide power failure in 2000:

> The government is drawing up urgent plans to prevent a millennium nightmare in which the start of 2000 is marked by power failures, flight problems and hospital disasters triggered by mass computer malfunction.
>
> Senior ministers fear privately that catastrophic damage may be caused by the "millennium time-bomb" the inability of many computers to deal with the change of date on January 1, 2000.
>
> However, critics claim neither the government nor the private sector is spending enough to defuse the potential catastrophe, and senior government sources confirm that much work needs to be done in case insufficient computer testing leads to disaster.
>
> "We have asked what is most important to society and come up with the answer that it is communication in the broadest sense," said one cabinet source. "Can we guarantee that traffic lights will work, that the roads will remain open, that ambulances can get through? What about power supplies? We have asked for work on all that."
>
> The concerns have been echoed by the NHS Confederation, which represents health trusts and authorities. It has submitted evidence to the Commons Science Select Committee inquiry into the

millennium timebomb, with the warning that the government must draw up contingency plans for a utilities breakdown and food shortages which could be caused if computer failure cripples distribution systems.

The confederation states boldly: "Contingency plans require development to address a possible scenario of major cities being without heat, clean water or transport, as well as shortages resulting from failed distribution systems."

— *Sunday Times* (February 15, 1998)

Many American Utilities Will Not Be Ready

We're no longer at the point of asking whether or not there will be any power disruptions, but we are now forced to ask how severe the disruptions are going to be.

— Senator Christopher Dodd (D-Conn.),
vice-chairman of the Senate committee on
the year 2000 problem (June 11, 1998)

There are 7800 power-generating and distribution organizations in the United States. On June 12, 1998, the Senate Y2K committee released a study that showed that of 10 of the nation's largest oil and gas utilities, serving 50 million people, none had a complete plan in case its computers failed because of the Y2K problem.

According to committee chairman Senator Robert Bennett, "Only two of the ten utilities had finished an assessment of their automated systems, which is an early step in the preparation process. One firm did not even know how many lines of computer code it had, and none had completed a Year 2000 contingency plan." As Senator

Bennett said in a classic, politically correct understatement, "The utilities preparations to ward off Year 2000 bugs are lagging."

A Y2K repair project is broken down into the following components: *Awareness* is 1 percent of the project; *Inventory* is 1 percent; *Assessment* is 5 percent; *Code Remediation* is 50–55 percent; and *Testing* is 40 percent of the repair project. According to the California White Paper on the Y2K compliance of America's power plants, released in February 1998, most utilities are not past the awareness/ inventory stage, leaving them with 98 percent of the repair project to complete. If one optimistically assumes said that by the end of the summer of 1998 all 7800 utilities had completed their assessment stage, that leaves only 500 days for the utilities to complete 93–95 percent of the Y2K work (remediation and testing).

Michael Gent, president of the North American Electric Reliability Counsel (NERC), told the Senate committee, "Year 2000 poses the threat that common mode failures . . . or the coincident loss of multiple facilities could result in stressing the electric system to the point of a cascading outage over a large area." With only a matter of months until the next century, senators on the committee said the prospects of fixing the power grid's millions of chips, microprocessors, computer programs, and other technologies are slim. Senator Dodd said, "If we don't have power to generate electricity, everything else is moot." When the Senate committee asked how prepared the utility industry is, Federal Energy Regulatory Commission chairman James Hocker said, "The state of the year 2000 readiness of the utility industry is largely unknown."

No Sense of Urgency Among the Utilities

On May 15, 1998, the Electric Power Research Institute, an organization that comprises the largest and most affluent U.S. utilities, met in Dallas. Most of the companies in attendance (under 100) were not finished with their assessments. If 100 percent of the largest, most affluent utilities are not beyond the assessment phase, what can we assume about the remaining 7700 utilities?

Rick Cowles, a computer expert with 17 years' experience in the electric power industry and a point man on reporting Y2K conditions in the industry, addressed this issue on February 27, 1998:

Most electric utilities are still, for the most part, in the awareness/inventory stage of Y2K. Some are actually still fighting about how to conduct inventory. There is very little upper management appreciation of the depth of the Y2K issue. That lack of appreciation translates into a significant deficit of executive-level support (resources and funding) for any Y2K projects. Y2K program managers are frustrated at their inability to convince their local or executive management that Y2K is, indeed, an enterprise-threatening problem. There is a sense of urgency at the Y2K program management level that is approaching panic, but the support is still not materializing.

Not one electric company has started a serious remediation effort on its embedded controls. Not one. Yes, there's been some testing going on, and a few pilot projects here and there, but for the most part it is still business-as-usual, as if there were 97 months to go, not 97 weeks.

Almost all electric utility projects are severely understaffed. I was at an independent generating company this week, which is responsible for production of nearly 3000 megawatts between just two large generating plants. This company still doesn't have a single full-time person dedicated to Y2K, and this includes the project manager. This is a USD $5 billion operation, and their management has committed only a few hundred thousand dollars of "seed money" to the project. I sincerely feel sympathy for the Y2K project manager. . . .

Oh, one other thing. Contingency plan? The industry hasn't started thinking about it yet. Here's my main message: the electric industry doesn't have the time left to lick this thing. It's not that the resources or ability aren't there; it's that the corporate will and executive-level understanding of the issue does not seem to be there. . . .

Rick Cowles has a web site, "Electric Utilities and the Year 2000" (http://www.2ktimebomb.com/PP/RC/rc9803.htm), that has excellent up-to-date information on Y2K remediation (or the lack thereof) in the electric power industry. He says we can be sure of major power failures in 2000.

As Gary North recently wrote, "If other nations' utilities are behind ours in Y2K awareness, which seems likely, then the world will lose its electric power. If national power grids stay down, the world goes back to

1850, but without the skills and tools we had in 1850, and with a vastly larger population."

Embedded Chips in the Public Utilities

Crawling among pipes and valves in manufacturing plants around the world, technicians wearing radio headsets are relaying to companions carrying portable computers the locations of digital time-bombs [embedded computer chips] ready to go off on the Ultimate Midnight on December 31, 1999. A massive hunt is on for the millions of computerized devices—machine tools, measuring instruments, computerized valves, and myriad other types of production equipment — whose software is tainted with the now infamous abbreviation "00."

Fortune (April 1998)

"From fossil-fuel plants to nuclear-power units, the electronics embedded in the power controls have become a major concern for utilities — even more of a concern than their business computer systems. Already, some utilities are reporting plant failures during tests that simulate the year 2000 date rollover," said Pete Valdellon, Year 2000 project coordinator for the Kissimmee Utilities Board.

The biggest problems that America's 7800 electric power utilities (coal, gas, nuclear and hydroelectric driven) face is not their computer mainframes, their software, or their PCs. It is the millions of embedded computer chips that are buried in power equipment. They are hard to find, and it is difficult to identify whether they are date-sensitive.

There are millions of embedded chips in our power stations, substations, and delivery systems' controls. Each one of these chips must be physically located, examined or tested, and replaced if necessary. Most power plants use thousands of these chips. One large petrochemical plant has 150,000 embedded chips.

Ed Medford, manager of Information Services for Knoxville Utilities Board, said the following in the *Knoxville News Sentinel* (September 21, 1997),

> Non-compliant embedded chips are buried in millions of systems — any of which may fail in 2000. It's a world-wide industry problem. Heavy 1980's reliance on embedded silicon microchips for storing dates and other data has left many businesses, including KUB and other utilities, vulnerable to far-reaching adverse effects if computer systems cannot comprehend year codes for 2000. Predictions are that millions of embedded microchips will fail in 1/1/2000, affecting everything from

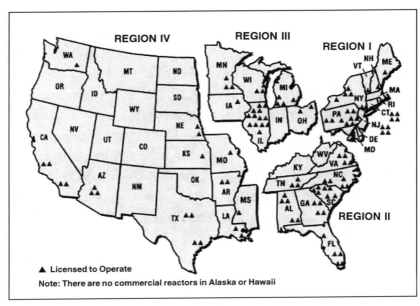

▲ Licensed to Operate

Note: There are no commercial reactors in Alaska or Hawaii

telephone systems and fax machines, to military messaging systems, the Global Positioning System, and coal, gas, hydroelectric and nuclear-powered electric plants.

The Vulnerability of the Nuclear Power Industry

The nation's 110 nuclear power plants account for 20–22 percent of the nation's electrical power. (See map of U.S. nuclear power plants.) In some regions of the country, the percentage is much greater (some parts of the eastern seaboard have over 50 percent of their power generated by nuclear power plants). The magnitude of the Y2K computer problem at nuclear power plants is huge. It encompasses virtually every area, administratively and operationally, of a nuclear facility. Hundreds of automatic controls and thousands of embedded chips exist through-out a typical nuclear power plant. Many data bases and maintenance scheduling computer programs are required for a plant to operate.

Unless a nuclear power plant can prove conclusively that the Y2K bug will not impact the safe operation of the plant or the ability to safely shut it down, the Nuclear Regulatory Commission (NRC) is mandated by the federal government to shut down the plants. The NRC is requiring a certification of year 2000 readiness from every nuclear power plant in America. This requirement is likely to be enforced no later than the third or fourth quarter of 1999. The NRC deadline for the completion of each power plant's Y2K projects is July 1, 1999.

Systems at Risk

Some examples of nuclear power plant systems and computer equipment that may be affected by Y2K problems include:

1. Plant process (data scan, log, and alarm and safety parameter display system) computers
2. Radiation monitoring systems
3. Dosimeters and readers
4. Plant simulators
5. Engineering programs
6. Communication systems
7. Inventory control systems
8. Surveillance and maintenance tracking systems
9. Control systems

In a recent memo to all U.S. nuclear power plants, the NRC warned that "control room display systems, radiation monitoring, and emergency response systems are particularly at risk."

> Diverse concerns are associated with the potential impact of the Y2K problem on nuclear power plants because of the variety and types of computer systems in use. The concerns result from licensees' reliance upon (1) software to schedule maintenance and technical specification surveillance; (2) programmable logic controllers and other commercial off-the-shelf software and hardware; (3) digital process control systems; (4) software to support facility operation; (5) digital systems for collection of operating data; and (6) digital systems to monitor post-accident plant conditions. . . .

U.S. Nuclear Power Plants in Perspective

In late 1997, Ed Yardeni testified to the Senate Banking Committee:

Some regions of the U.S. rely on nuclear power stations for half of their power. These plants are not Y2K compliant.

There are 110 licensed nuclear power plants generating 22 percent of the nation's electricity. Three of the six major regions of the country depend on nuclear power for at least one-quarter of their electricity. Six states — Connecticut, New Jersey, Maine, Vermont, South Carolina, and Illinois — rely on nuclear power for more than half their electricity.

More than 80 nuclear plants have gone on line since 1973 and they accounted for 40 percent of the increase in U.S. electricity demand since then. More than 30 nations rely on nuclear energy for a portion of their electricity supply. In 1996, the 442 nuclear power plants operating in the world generated one-sixth of the total electricity produced on the planet. Western Europe depends on nuclear energy for about 42 percent of its electricity. Japan is at 35 percent. East Asia is at 17 percent.

Concern Growing in the Nuclear Power Industry

On June 20, 1998, the *National Journal* wrote the following:

No one in the nuclear power industry wants to talk publicly about the worst that could happen come midnight December 31, 1999, when the clocks in the thousands of technical systems deep within the nation's 110 nuclear power plants roll over to the year 2000.

Behind the scenes, however, industry officials are scrambling to prevent their safety mechanisms from failing and triggering a nuclear meltdown. The Nuclear Regulatory Commission (NRC) has been working with utilities since 1996 to identify and solve any computer-related power plant problems. But just to be sure, most electric companies are likely to temporarily shut down their nuclear plants in the days before the millennium, according to Rick Cowles, manager of the Y2K program for Digital Equipment Corp., a Massachusetts-based computer firm.

"The potential for liability is so enormous that there will be very few nuclear power plant executives willing to say their company is Year 2000-compliant," Cowles said.

Jim Lord, editor of the *Year 2000 Survival Newsletter*, and computer consultant to the U.S. Defense Department and other government agencies on the Y2K problem, recently wrote the following:

I am adding Electrical Utilities to the Greatest Risk list. I believe there is a strong possibility of disruptions in the nation's electrical grid. I have received information that some utilities companies are so far behind, that they know they cannot get done in time so their current strategy is to prepare as much favorable evidence as possible for the inevitable lawsuits. They are doing this by building up a nice stack of paper proving they tried as hard as they could.

My expectation is that 15 percent or so of the fossil-fueled electrical generating plants will shut down because of disruptions in the delivery of fuel (mostly coal). Problems with embedded processors in the rail transportation system will be the most likely culprit.

Much worse will be the eventual shutdown of all nuclear power plants in the country. This will be mandated by the Nuclear Regulatory Commission (NRC) when it becomes clear that the safety of the plants cannot be guaranteed.

Interestingly, the NRC has no charter to deliver power to the public. Their job is solely to oversee nuclear safety. Eventually, the environmental movement will catch on to the environmental dangers posed by Y2K. They will enlist the aid of Vice President Gore, who will pressure the NRC to close down the plants rather than taking the risk. When a few of these secondary systems fail, it will become a done deal.

Nuclear power accounts for about 22 percent of all electricity generated and 40 percent on the eastern seaboard. From what I can determine, there is very little likelihood of nuclear accidents because most of the reactors are so old they are not heavily automated.

The operation of the plants is very dependent, however on more modern (and more susceptible) systems used to manage secondary functions such as radiation monitoring or plant security access and control.

The combined effect of these shutdowns will be widespread brownouts and blackouts across the United States and Canada followed by a massive public outcry for the federal government to "do something," followed by nation-wide power rationing. My guess is this will continue for six to nine months as the grid is slowly brought into Y2K compliance and full service. It will not be a happy time. It will not, however, be a return to the Dark Ages — just the Dim Ages.

Russian Nuclear Power Plants at Risk

Western intelligence is warning of a possible nuclear "meltdown" in the former Soviet bloc countries as a result of the millennium bug. Intelligence sources say some of the 65 Soviet-made civilian nuclear power plants are likely to malfunction as their computers fall victim to Y2K. Russia has 29 civilian nuclear reactors, 11 of which are similar to the Chernobyl reactor, which released 200 times as much radioactivity as the atomic bombs at Hiroshima and Nagasaki. The other 36 reactors are in former Soviet-Bloc countries. Western experts believe that many are already unsafe.

Russia's nuclear industry is in desperate straits. There is a severe shortage of computer experts to work on the problem. If Russian plants malfunction, the effects will be felt all over the former Soviet Union and in western Europe as well. It should also be noted that Cuba has

Russian-built Chernobyl-type reactors. Residents of South Florida should contemplate the implications of this fact.

Two Factors That Will Compound the Y2K Impact on U.S. Electric Power Utilities

It is noteworthy that two factors are emerging to compound the Y2K impact on U.S. electrical power: 1) deregulation of the industry, and 2) a wave of solar storms that will hit in 2000.

Deregulation

Whenever an industry goes through deregulation, it goes through a period of instability and disorganization. According to a report in *Infoworld* (January 19, 1998), the looming deregulation, and commencement of a two-way transmission of power, wherein states are deregulating their electric utility systems, will create chaos at the same time that Y2K will hit a weakened, disrupted system. It is analogous to the Eurocurrency changeover, which is taking place at the same time that Europe is trying to do its Y2K remediation. Governments are trying to do two things at once, neither of which could be effectively done in the small amount of time remaining. *Infoworld* reported the following:

> Sags, surges, spikes, brownouts, and power outages will become a more common occurrence in the lives of IS managers in the coming year. As states begin to deregulate their electric utility markets, industry and government officials are predicting that rock-steady electricity service is in peril, particularly in the short term.

Energy industry deregulation is meant to introduce

competition into the market and ultimately lower prices, but industry and government officials are predicting that industry confusion and the technical limitations of power grids will likely mean shakier service, experts say. "The risk is, as we go through this competitive restructuring, critical information must be broadly and rapidly shared between generators and transmission owners," says Bruce Humphrey, director of research at Cambridge Energy Research Associates, a consulting information company for the energy industry in Cambridge, Mass. "That has not yet been tested...."

The grid has never had to handle on an hourly basis the thousands of two-way transactions wherein electric power is bought and sold, sometimes at auction, by businesses and power-generation companies. The generation of power is also being restructured. Each state will have its own way of doing it, but the purpose is to allow individuals and companies to buy power from competing suppliers. From the DOE down the line, everyone appears to believe that in the long run power will be less expensive. But it is in the short run, estimated to last from one to eight quarters depending on who answers the question, that there may be an increase in power outages, brownouts, surges, spikes, and sags....

Applegate's Jim Mack says, "There is a fundamental problem that engineers talk about. The grid was not designed for two-way trading. The potential for the complexity of the system borders on chaos," says Ann-Marie Borbely, manager of the Energy Services Research Unit at Frost and Sullivan, in Mountain View, California. "Can the system handle multiple alarms? No one knows." A member of the California Public Utilities Commission (CPUC) doesn't dispute some of those concerns. "There is an element of truth that two-way transmission was not designed for the power grid," says Marc Ziering, manager in the Energy Division of the CPUC.

Solar Flare Storms

The power grid is subject to sharp fluctuations in times of solar flare storms. The next wave of such storms will hit in 2000. John Kappenman, who is in charge of Transmission Power Engineering at Minnesota Power, in Duluth, Minnesota, wrote the following in the May 1996 issue of *IEEE Power Engineering Review:*

> Solar Cycle 22 (the current 11-year sunspot cycle) which is now drawing to a close, produced not only above-average, but historic high levels of geomagnetic storm activity. As a consequence, above-average impacts to electrical system reliability occurred due to storms, with the most notable instance resulting in a large area blackout. Also, several well-documented cases convincingly established that large, expensive transformers could be damaged by exposure to Geomagnetically Induced Currents (GIC) that are produced by solar storms.

> Further, statistical evidence is showing that transformers are failing at an above-average rate in areas of the United States that are particularly prone to

geomagnetic disturbances, resulting in well-above-average replacement costs. If that's not enough, experience teaches us that the odd-numbered Solar Cycles (Cycle 23 in this case, which is in the process of initiating) have always been more severe than the even-numbered cycles that they follow.

Threats to power system integrity are no longer just academic speculation with the events that unfolded during the Great Geomagnetic Storm of March 13, 1989. In fact, the entire Hydro Quebec system was plunged into a blackout triggered by GIC-caused voltage collapse and equipment malfunction. The impact of this particular storm was simultaneously felt over the entire North American continent, with most of Hydro Quebec's neighboring systems in the United States coming uncomfortably close to experiencing the same sort of voltage collapse/cascading outage scenario. . . . Wide area blackouts are the nightmare scenario of our industry and geomagnetic storms that span large regions of the network impose a unique and previously unanticipated threat to interconnected system operation. . . .

During the same March 1989 storm, several incidents of transformer heating problems were reported as well. The most significant failure occurred at a GSU (generation step-up) transformer at a nuclear plant in New Jersey in which a 1,200 MVA, 500kV bank was damaged beyond repair. . . .

It is an interesting coincidence that the next major solar flare storm will hit in the year 2000, compounding and exacerbating an already highly stressed power grid. Like the "rogue wave" discussed in an earlier chapter, the Y2K computer meltdown, power company deregulation, and a new solar flare storm will all hit about the same time. What will be the impact on U.S. power plants?

The Vulnerability of the Natural Gas Industry to Y2K

Natural gas is essential to America's energy and electric power industry. The gas industry is not presently Y2K compliant nor will it be, by its own admission, until October 1999, providing all goes well. Paul Slish, a computer expert who has worked for 15 years for National Fuel Gas as a programmer, systems analyst, and database administrator, made the following assessment of America's natural gas — its exploration, production, transmission, storage, and distribution:

> Natural gas is a major energy source in the United States. Natural gas accounts for 31 percent of energy production and 25 percent of energy consumption in the United States. More than 50 percent of the energy consumed by residential and commercial customers is supplied by natural gas. Natural gas provides 41 percent of the energy used by U.S. industry; 27 percent of this production comes from offshore areas.

> Ninety-nine percent of the natural gas consumed is produced in North America. There are more than 60 million residential and commercial natural gas customers in the United States. This totals 175,000,000 American consumers. Fifty-three percent of American homes use natural gas for a total of 59 million. In the United States, there are 288,000 producing natural gas wells, 125 natural gas

pipeline companies, and 1200 gas distribution companies. The transmission and main distribution pipelines total 1,300,000 miles. The United States accounts for 24 percent of the world's annual natural gas production. Seventeen percent of the natural gas consumed in the United States is used to produce electric power. This represents 11 percent of the electric power generated.

There are basically five segments of the industry: exploration, production, transmission, storage, and distribution. Obviously, if there is any significant disruption, even in the short run, to production, transmission, or distribution of natural gas, it would wreak havoc in the lives of residential consumers, and to the operations of most of the commercial and industrial concerns in the United States. Any lengthy disruption to either exploration or storage (either incoming or outgoing) would also wreak havoc on the U.S. economy.

No particular transmission pipeline or distribution company runs its system in isolation from other pipelines. In fact, there is an integrated North American natural gas production, transmission, storage, and distribution system. As noted earlier, there are 1,300,000 miles of transmission and main distribution pipelines in North America. Gas is moved from the southwestern United States to the highly populated eastern United States by about four major pipeline companies. The Trans-Canada pipeline ties in with U.S. pipeline companies in the northern United States. For example,

Trans-Canada ties in with National Fuel's system at Lewiston, New York. Specifically, they meet at the bottom of the Niagara River halfway across.

Therefore, any significant shutdown of the production system would within a few days severely impact the transmission and distribution systems. A shutdown in any of the major transmission pipelines would quickly impact the remainder of the transmission system and the distribution system. Problems with withdrawals at any significant number of storage fields in the middle of winter would have a large impact on the distribution system.

With the high level of use of PCs, network servers, and process logic controllers in all segments of the natural gas industry, the possibility of various Y2K failures taking place once January 1, 2000, is reached is high. The millennium bug could possibly hit the natural gas production transmission, distribution, and storage network quite hard. Why does this writer come to this conclusion?

As mentioned earlier, there are 288,000 gas wells, 125 pipeline companies, and 1,200 distribution companies in the United States. Who is coordinating Y2K repairs among all these producers, transmitters, and distributors? There is no group or managerial body systematically doing this. The Interstate Natural Gas Association and the Gas Research Institute are both conducting surveys of their members, according to Kathleen Hirning, the CIO of FERC. Surveys are very initial steps.

Some of these companies may be doing very well in

remediating their computer systems for Y2K compliance. Others, however, may not be. The question is, who knows? How many pipeline companies need to experience Y2K-related failures, before the overall transmission system is substantially impacted? Recall that natural gas accounts for 25 percent of the energy consumed in the United States. I find it astounding that as of mid-1998 there is no managerial body comprehensively measuring the progress of Y2K remediation in the nationwide natural gas industry, let alone prodding laggard companies into increased action or any action at all.

Recall also that 17 percent of natural gas produced is used to generate electricity. Eleven percent of electric energy is produced in this fashion. Failures in the natural gas transmission and distribution network could heavily impact electricity generation. Conversely, the natural gas system could not be sustained for any length of time if there are long-term electrical power outages. There is backup electricity-generation capabilities in many instances, but it is not designed for long-term usage of weeks or months. At this time, the writer cannot forecast one way or the other whether the natural gas system will perform reliably come January 1, 2000. *Natural Gas: A Vital But Noncompliant Industry* (May 19, 1998)

The full text of Paul Slish's article on the natural gas industry and its vulnerability to Y2K can be read on Gary North's web site (http://www.garynorth.com/Y2K/detail).

It appears that only part of the natural gas industry will be Y2K compliant. Can the noncompliant part pull down the compliant part — especially if there are other problems in the power grid around the United States?

Why Many Power Stations Will Shut Down

"If Y2K hit tomorrow, there is a 100 percent chance that the grid would fail. With 18 months to go, we may be able to get this down to 40 percent." Senator Robert Bennett (R-Utah), chairman of the Senate committee on the Y2K problem (June 9, 1998).

There are over 7,800 power companies in the United States. As of August 1998, not one is certified to be compliant. Over 40 percent of U.S. power plants are coal-fired. They all depend on railroad shipments of coal, and there are no compliant railroads in America. The switching systems that control traffic are computerized and noncompliant, and the computers are so specialized that only a handful of programmers can fix them. At fossil fuel-powered plants the temperature and monitoring devices are date-sensitive, and they could shut down plants. Transmission/power supply, the system that automatically sends power out at the right time and date, could malfunction.

If the supplier of power equipment and spare parts is in a region where the grid fails, it will not be able to supply these items to power plants that survive the shutdown by pulling off the grid in 2000. Where will the surviving utilities get their spare parts? A typical power plant has 6,000 separate items it relies upon.

In May 1998, Joseph Sgroi, a computer specialist with intimate knowledge of the U.S. electrical system and power grid, wrote the following report for the Cassandra Project:

> There is a high probability of severe long-term power blackouts as a result of noncompliant real-time embedded systems failing within the power station environment in the year 2000.
>
> It is now becoming apparent that most power stations have not yet reached the point where a thorough, detailed, Y2K Business Risk Assessment has been performed. Specifically, there has not been enough evidence to indicate that the following items have been addressed in a detailed, adequate manner:
>
> 1) A full inventory of I.T. systems, real-time systems, and date-dependent components and equipment that are on the critical path to producing power at a power station.
>
> 2) Identified, and confirmed with detailed tests, which of the above items will fail in the year 2000.
>
> 3) Provided detailed cost, time, and resource estimates for the replacement of the above.
>
> Unfortunately, time will not stand still while we complete the above.
>
> The harsh reality is that on all conservative estimates, there could be somewhere between 100–400 components or items of equipment that are not compliant at a power station and are likely to fail. In most instances, failure will result in that item of equipment shutting itself down, which in turn

causes the power station to shut down, or a failure in another embedded component down the chain. Evidence to this effect is now starting to emerge on the Internet.

Can all of these components be identified, tested, and replaced in 18 months? The task is made more difficult, as many of these components are purpose-built for a particular power station, with unique specifications, where the documentation may or may not be currently available. What about the suppliers of these components? Are they still in operation? The enormity of this conundrum starts to take shape in our minds. There are four indisputable facts with this critical problem:

1) All power stations that are not compliant in the year 2000 will cease producing electricity.

2) Once they are down, they will stay down for a very long time — until their non-compliant components, equipment and I.T. systems are replaced.

3) Most, if not all, power stations will be affected by the Y2K problem.

4) The year 2000 problem will strike most, if not all, power stations at the same time.

Y2K will hit most, if not all, power stations at the same time. This, as a minimum, would cause blackouts of weeks or months. In the worst case, a system blackout could result that would be a catastrophe. Either scenario would result in severe social disruption with major impacts to the well-being of our society and our own families.

Once a power station goes down in the rollover to year 2000, the harsh reality is that those small time batteries on the non-compliant circuit boards within components and equipment will guarantee that the incorrect date is maintained on that component or item of equipment. So even if we can kick-start that station with a backup generator, the non-compliant components will again cause that power station to shut down. The power station remains unusable until *all* non-compliant components and items of equipment are replaced.

There may not be enough time to investigate, test and replace approximately 100–400 items of equipment in each power station and complete all this work within 18 months. Even if we manage to find suppliers for all our components that are to be replaced, the inter-equipment interface specifications and operational functionality, along with the necessary tests, would be the issue here, which would cause unacceptable delays in time.

What to Do When the Lights Go Out: A Case Study in Urban Blackout. The Ice Storm of January 1998

The following letter from Charles E. St. James describes what can happen when the electric power goes down in your town or city:

On January 7th, 1998, Watertown, New York experienced a devastating ice storm. We lost our power on January 8, 1998 at approximately 8:30 a.m. With our home being all electric, this meant no heat, water, or lights. Initially, we thought we would only be without power for a couple of days, but days turned into weeks (three weeks to be exact).

Fortunately for us, we had a wood stove, so we were able to keep plenty warm and do all our cooking on top of the stove. As for drinking water, we had filled a few two-liter bottles of water the night before, but this would only last a couple of days. Our neighbors had a pool that provided us with water to flush the toilet and bathe, but only after chiseling through about six inches of ice on the surface of the pool!

Candles and oil lamps provided our light. Our only link to the outside world was a portable radio for those of us who had batteries! Our phone lines were also down, and little did we know at the time that they would be down for about a month. Families weren't able to get through to see if their relatives were all right, which caused a lot of anxiety.

Our refrigerator only kept the food cool for a few days, and then we had to become resourceful and find ways to try to save whatever food we had. We gathered ice from the outdoors and put it in coolers.

No travel was allowed during the first few days because there were too many power lines and trees down, which made it just too dangerous. Until the driving ban was lifted, we had to make do with what supplies we had on hand. Neighbors looked in on each other and shared whatever they had. We had plenty of wood, as we had bought for the whole season, but our neighbors were coming to us for wood for their families, which depleted our household supply. If this crisis had gone on long enough, our household would have been without wood for heat also.

As the days turned into weeks, supplies were getting low. Once the driving ban was lifted we were able to venture into the city and seek out stores that were open. Those that were open, allowed only a few people in at a time. This was no easy task as the lines were long and stores were also running low on batteries, candles, kerosene, etc., as they were unable to get their shipments.

Trucks from other states were bringing in supplies, but then there was the problem of price gouging! Money was also running low in many households because banks were not open and there were no ATMs. People were unable to go to work, which resulted in lost wages. We personally own our business and were not able to open. When we did, most of our customers were staying with families out of the area and, therefore, we lost a lot of our business.

A 5:00 p.m. curfew was also put into effect so that the work crew could work on restoring the power as well as to prevent looting. Anyone found walking on the streets or driving their cars were ticketed.

Many people who were not as fortunate as we were to own a wood stove or other source of heat were forced to leave their homes and go into shelters. This caused a lot of anxiety because most people don't want to have to leave their homes if at all possible.

After a week of having no power, we resorted to a generator (which is what a lot of people were doing) but the supply just couldn't meet the demand so it took awhile to find one. Many people had their generators stolen from their yards as they had to be installed outside because of the fumes. Those of us who had generators had to take caution to safeguard them.

Lesson: The unprepared will plunder and steal from the prepared in a crisis. So, as much as possible, keep your preparations very private — except with family and close friends!

One would think that during times like this, more people would turn to the Lord in prayer. Many did; however, most people felt they were in control and thought praying to the Lord was foolishness.

One lesson we learned through this ordeal was how dependent we are on power companies and how we take for granted such easy access to food sources, gasoline, kerosene, and water supplies. Another lesson we learned was to be prepared for such disasters!

What if that had been in a major city instead of a small town? What if the blackout had lasted for weeks? What if the family had had no source of heat? What if a whole state or region, or God forbid, the whole country had been involved in the blackout? What can we learn from this family's experience? For more information on the three-week Watertown blackout, contact Charles E. St. James (email: cesdjs@northnet.org)

9

Transportation Systems at Risk: Railroads and Airlines

The Impact of the Y2K Crisis on Railroad Transportation

The operational nightmare the Union Pacific Railroad is going through in its inept attempt to integrate its computer system with that of the recently acquired Southern Pacific is just one example of the crippling gridlock that is likely to eventuate from Y2K problems in advanced electronically integrated economies like ours.

— Edward Yardeni, in an interview with *Barron's* (November 3, 1997)

The average American, who rarely rides a train, has no idea how dependent the United States is on railroads. Most large cities are primarily fed, warmed, and provisioned by railroads. Railroads today do most of the heavy hauling of such raw materials and staples as coal, petro-leum, heating oil, chemicals, food. Millions of container-size truckbeds loaded with finished goods are hauled by rail. Just one railroad, Union Pacific, moves 350,000 carloads of freight on a normal day.

If the railroads, which depend heavily on computers, go down due to Y2K noncompliance, the lights will go out, the fuel will dry up, and we will run out of food — especially in large or medium-sized American cities. To make matters worse, of all American industries, the rail-roads are among those most behind in Y2K repairs.

We don't normally associate computers with railroads, but computers schedule and signal trains to get them to their location on time; they keep trains from running into each other while en route; they operate track switching mechanisms; and they track the exact location and move-ment of over a million rail cars (boxcars, tankers, flatbeds, top- and bottom-loading cars for wheat, corn, soybeans, coal, sulfur, fertilizer, plastics, and a host of chemicals, upon which industry is dependent).

For the railroads to operate, all their computers must communicate with competitor railroads, suppliers, and customers. If they can't interface, due to the Y2K problem, the trains will stop, the rail system will go into gridlock, and the U.S. economy will grind to a halt. Each rail car has a number on its side that is entered into a mainframe computer that routes and keeps track of the movement and location of that car. These cars, often owned by indi-vidual investors, are often transferred to other railroads, and the mainframe computers that regulate their move-ments may be thousands of miles away from the trains they control.

Until 20 years ago, train orders were typically written out in longhand and sent over an open telephone line from a dispatcher. These orders, which governed train movement, were handed up to passing trains, and the switches that change a train's direction were operated manually through a tower interlocking plant. The entire system was manual; it was simple. It was labor intensive, but it worked.

Then railroad management decided to cut labor costs by adopting state-of-the-art computer technology to eliminate all of the operators and levermen. They decided to issue train orders via radio transmission directly to the train crew. Train crews were cut from four to two (an engineer and a conductor), and all the old switching towers were torn down and replaced with sophisticated electronics linked to the dispatcher by regular telephone lines. Today there is no manual switching.

If the Y2K bug affects computers, the national power supply, and the telephone companies (as it is very likely to do), the nation's rail lines will grind to a sudden halt. If trains cannot receive their right-of-way train orders, no engineer or conductor will move his train an inch. To move a train without authority from a dispatcher would invite a disastrous train wreck.

Union Pacific: A Case Study in Transcontinental Rail Gridlock

Union Pacific is the largest railroad in the country. It has 53,000 employees and carries 350,000 carloads of freight on a normal day. By its own description, Union Pacific is "one of North America's leading transportation, computer technology, and logistics companies, with operations in all 50 states, Canada, and Mexico." Union Pacific has developed a highly integrated system (totally computer dependent) that controls all aspects of railroad operation, including the following:

1. Billing and rating
2. Car and train movement
3. Empty-car distribution
4. Freight-car scheduling
5. Yard classification and inventory control
6. Locomotive scheduling and maintenance
7. Crew dispatching
8. Work-order management
9. Interline shipment monitoring

In 1995, Union Pacific discovered that it had a Y2K problem in the software programs that handle five-year scheduling, budgeting, and forecasting. They initially identified 12 million lines of code that needed to be repaired. A company analysis revealed that 82.5 percent of the programs had date-related fields: 7,000 COBOL programs needed to be fixed — requiring about 200,000 man-hours.

However, in July 1997, Union Pacific management acknowledged that only about 6 percent of its repairs were completed after two years of work on the project. At the present rates of repair, none of the railroads (including Union Pacific) will be Y2K compliant by December 31, 1999.

How did Union Pacific get distracted from its Y2K compliance repairs for two years? In 1996, Union Pacific acquired the Southern Pacific Railroad and began to try to integrate the highly complex and diverse computer systems of the two railroads. Integrating the two has been a nightmare, according to Union Pacific spokesmen. The merger and resultant computer gridlock have been a disaster for Union Pacific and for the entire U.S. railroad system. The problems they encountered provide a very useful example of the kind of gridlock that is likely to occur after January 1, 2000.

The *San Francisco Chronicle* (October 11, 1997) carried an article entitled "Transcontinental Rail Gridlock — Merging of SP, UP Tracks Creates a Train Bottleneck," that illustrates the vulnerability of these (and all other) U.S. railroads:

> When Union Pacific swallowed the San Francisco - ased Southern Pacific last year, it hoped the result would be the nation's biggest — and perhaps best — railroad. Instead the merger is choking the UP and spreading chaos throughout the nation's rail system. It is the corporate merger from hell. The well-regarded Union Pacific took over the ailing Southern Pacific last year for $3.9 billion, but when it tried to put the two systems together the SP's problems spilled out of control over the larger line.

> The result was rail gridlock that began with paralysis in a switching yard in Houston last summer and spread all over the West like a disease. Now it is affecting coal shipments in Colorado, grain in the Midwest, shipments of frozen french fries from Idaho to Japan, automobile parts, Amtrak passenger trains, even shipping containers full of stuffed animal toys bound from China for the Christmas market. It all moves by rail — or did. The Union Pacific is the largest railroad in the history of the

country and carries 350,000 carloads of freight on a normal day.

The railroad says the southern corridor — from Los Angeles to Texas and the Midwest, has the worst logjam, but it also says jams extend on what it calls the central corridor, from the Bay Area to the Midwest, and up and down the coast as far north as Seattle. "The problems are all over. We're seeing delays of anywhere between 10 and 30 days," said David McLean, director of marketing for Circle International, a San Francisco freight forwarding company that arranges transportation for other businesses.

The ports of Los Angeles and Long Beach, the biggest in the country and heavily dependent on UP's unit trains, are jammed with cargo that can't move. . . .

"The UP is in chaos," said Brian Rosenwald, a Los Angeles-based Amtrak executive. The system's main lines are jammed with trains that can't move because of a lack of rail yard space, a lack of locomotives, or a lack of train crews. It is, said one former Southern Pacific executive, "a virus that is spreading out of control."

Some shippers say it is taking a month to move a freight car from the West Coast to Texas. There is a backlog of 30,000 freight containers in Los Angeles/Long Beach harbors. . . .

"It started in mid-June, grew over the summer, was significant by August and extremely serious by the

Labor Day weekend," UP spokesman John Bromley said. In effect, even the company admits the problem spiraled out of control. As of yesterday [10/10/97], the Union Pacific was so jammed up, it wanted to move 40,000 railroad cars off the system onto other rails — enough to make up a freight train nearly 500 miles long.

The railroad has submitted what it calls "a recovery plan" to the Surface Transportation Board, but admits it will take at least 90 days to straighten the problem out. . . .

Union Pacific has found it almost impossible to merge its computer system with Southern Pacific's different system. In Kansas and other Midwest grain-producing states, the rail service deteriorated so badly last fall that in Kansas alone, 24 million bushels of grain were never picked up by the railroad and delivered to market. Much of that grain did not get to market for six to eight months.

The Y2K Impact on Air Transportation

There are 169,000 airline takeoffs and landings in America each day by thousands of airliners at hundreds of U.S. airports. Large airliners like the Boeing 747 or 767 or McDonnell-Douglas MD-11 can have up to 500 computers in operation on board (as well as tens of thousands of computer chips) that perform takeoff, landing, collision detection, navigation, communications with air controllers, and numerous other functions.

On November 11, 1997, KLM Royal Dutch Airlines became the first airline to state officially that it may ground some of its aircraft because of the Y2K problem. KLM said it would consider halting some flights on

January 1, 2000, because of potential systems failures caused by the century changeover. *Reuters* reported that KLM is also concerned about computer systems both inside and outside the airport.

The FAA's Air Traffic Control System

The FAA air traffic control system is one of the nation's largest and most complex computer systems; it is also one of the oldest, and has been the subject of a major redesign and redevelopment for the past several years. As of early 1998, FAA software and mainframes were not Y2K compliant. The Department of Transportation, which runs the FAA and the nation's Air Traffic Control radar, was not even scheduled to be finished with their assessments until December 1997, mostly because their initial assessment tripled the amount of work initially estimated. In 1997 the General Accounting Office estimated that the Department of Transportation computers will not be fixed until the year 2003 at the present rate of repair.

The *New York Times* (January 13, 1998) carried the following article entitled "Year 2000 Raises Safety Risk for Air Traffic Computers":

> A set of crucial computers in the nation's air traffic control system should not be used beyond December 1999, because they may not operate reliably when the date rolls over to January 1, 2000, and there is no way to predict the effect on air traffic, according to IBM, which built the computers.

> But the official in charge of that system at the Federal Aviation Administration said on Monday that "it would be an extraordinary feat" to replace about 40 mainframe computers by then. Instead,

his agency, with the help of a retired IBM programmer and a team of software experts, is racing to determine whether the problems can be anticipated and eliminated before the turn of the century.

The extent of problems with the air traffic computers is not certain, but experts say that the #3083 mainframe model referred to in a letter from IBM to an FAA contractor, might, for example, refuse to accept flight plans for planes that take off on December 31, 1999, and land on Jan. 1. That landing would be 99 years in the past, from the computer's point of view.

Already, FAA teams have found, deep in the computer code, a monthly command that enables a computer to switch from one cooling pump to another; if it is not fixed, experts say, routine could stop running, allowing the computers to overheat and fail if the pump breaks down. In fact, experts say, there could be many such land mines — buried in millions of lines of computer code — that could cause failures for days, weeks or months after the new year.

"We're kind of worried about it," said Jack Ryan, a former FAA manager who is now the air traffic control expert at the Air Transport Association, the trade association of the major airlines. "I think the FAA has the right sense of urgency, although it's a little bit late."

The computers in question are at the 20 Air Route Traffic Control Centers, which handle all the high-altitude, long-distance traffic in the country.

The 3083 models were once common in business and industry but few remain in service, experts say. IBM stopped shipping them about 10 years ago, but some of the software on the FAA models is even older, dating from the early 1970s.

The FAA has 250 separate computer systems, most of which will require fixes but the 3083 is the only one that IBM says can't be debugged before 2000.

The problem, known among information technology experts as Y2K, for the year 2000, is hardly unique to the FAA. But it is especially acute there, because the air traffic control system demands an extremely high level of reliability and because the FAA cannot bypass the software built into the 3083s that has the date problem by simply running the air traffic programs on new computers.

In the October letter from IBM to the FAA contractor Lockheed Martin Air Traffic Management, it said, "IBM remains convinced that the appropriate skills and tools do not exist to conduct a complete Year 2000 test assessment" of the 3083 computers. "IBM believes it is imperative that the FAA replace the equipment" before 2000.

Ryan, of the Air Traffic Association, says the larger problem is that no one knows what else lurks in the 30-year-old software. "I don't know what I don't know, and that's what's very worrisome about it," he said.

If the ATC radars go down for long, air traffic will cease. At busy terminals such as Los Angeles

International, large jets take off or land several times a minute around the clock, regardless of weather. Aircraft must be sequenced and guided by radar and time-reliant computers with clocklike precision to prevent disaster even while they are on the ground. If such services are halted, all aircraft will be grounded.

Businesses around the country depend on "just-in-time" delivery of parts from these craft, many of which come from hundreds of different countries. Those hundreds of other countries each have their own ATC radar systems, all mirroring our own. If their radars are not also fixed, then international cargo and passenger flights will be impossible.

Why Is Air Transportation at Risk from the Y2K Crisis?

If the power grid and telephone/telecommunications are the two most important elements of our economy and infrastructure with regard to Y2K, air transportation must be a close third. Forget about personal and business air travel, which has become a way of life for all of us in recent years. The more critical aspect of air transport is the moving of mail and boxes by the U.S. Post Office, UPS, Federal Express, DHL, and the increasing number of "just-in-time" deliveries of equipment to U.S. businesses. Without these deliveries, many businesses would grind to a halt.

The FAA Is Way Behind

There is deep concern in and out of the government that the FAA (which runs the nation's air traffic control system) is in serious trouble with respect to Y2K compliance. The FAA originally believed it could fix all its mission-critical computers by November 1999, but as of April 8, 1998, independent auditors estimated that only 29 of 430 FAA computer systems are fixed; that's less than 7 percent. The National Civil Aviation Review Commission has warned that the nation could face aviation gridlock severe enough to severely damage the U.S. economy and shut down the air traffic control network responsible for monitoring tens of thousands of flights each day.

Recently, the General Accounting Office released a very critical report on the FAA's inadequate response to Y2K, pointing out that "delays in completing the awareness and assessment phases of the project leave FAA little time for critical renovation, validation, and implementation activities." Rep. Bart Gordon (R-TN) said regarding the GAO report, "The country could be left at a standstill and that could be devastating."

Concern is spreading, as demonstrated by a recent poll done by *CIO* magazine, which said that 41 percent of business executives won't fly on January 1, 2000. That will probably grow to 98 percent by December 1999. Readers are strongly encouraged to get your necessary air travel out of the way well before that time frame. The FAA is so far behind in its Y2K fixes that its 2000 fixes won't be completed until mid-2009, according to Stanley Graham, a consultant at Tech-Beamers, Inc. in Poughkeepsie, New York, who testified before Congressional hearings regarding the FAA.

The FAA's program manager claimed in April that 125 of 209 critical systems in the National Aerospace System are compliant, leaving only 84 that require modification. However, "compliant" has come to mean "we're working on it." What remains to be seen is whether the 84 remaining systems can be corrected in time, and whether or not the 48 ATC traffic control centers in the country are included in that number. The FAA admits that a major thrust will be required to make those 84 systems compliant.

Will the Aircraft Be Compliant?

Meanwhile, there is concern that aircraft flying in the U.S. may not be Y2K compliant. Large U.S. jumbo jets can have hundreds of computers and thousands of embedded chips on board. At risk are some of the sophisticated navigational and flight control systems that have been introduced into cockpits in the last 15 years. Mid-air crashes, missed runways, and aborted takeoffs could occur if the avionics are not compliant. Boeing says that its most recent models and its very early jets are not affected by Y2K, but that their in-between aircraft need some attention.

Airline Radar in Northeast Fails Frequently

Investor's Business Daily (June 19, 1998) recently reported that "radar screens used by air traffic controllers in New England and upstate New York go blank or freeze almost daily, the controllers' union told the *Boston Globe*. A computer system installed in 1972 causes outages of up to 2½ hours and more technicians are needed to keep it working. The FAA said the system is safe and it has no record of daily failures. Controllers use a backup system and radio communications as a last resort."

Aviation Industry Union Says
Air Traffic Control System Will Be Unsafe

The *New York Times* (May 23, 1998) wrote:

A billion-dollar air traffic control system that is scheduled to start service next spring will jeopardize air safety, the union representing the technicians who will maintain it says, because it lacks alarms and monitoring systems to give warning when it is beginning to fail.

In addition, the Federal Aviation Administration is not sure that the new software, which will not enter service until 1999 at the earliest, will function properly after the calendar rolls over to 2000.

The union, the Professional Airways Systems Specialists, is seeking a delay in the phase-in, which is scheduled to begin in March 1999 at Washington National Airport.

The electronics technicians say that if a processing glitch makes the air traffic system briefly lose track of an airplane in flight, the equipment currently in use will sound a shrill alarm and flash lights indicating the source of the problem. In the new system, if a controller were not watching that blip at that moment, the failure could go undetected until a problem became "catastrophic," which would mean an accident or a computer collapse, the union says.

Officials at the aviation agency belatedly agree that a better alarm system would be desirable, but they say it is important to put new equipment in the field because the existing technology is falling apart.

There are plans to install this questionable new system

at Washington National, New York (JFK and LaGuardia) and Dallas–Fort Worth Airports in 1999.

Major U.S. Airports May Not Be Y2K Compliant

On April 19, 1998, the *Associated Press* reported that the $4.3 billion Denver International Airport (DIA), which opened in February 1995, billed as the most modern airport in the world ("the state-of-the-art airport of the 21st century"), is noncompliant on 100 different systems. Of those, 40 systems have been deemed "mission critical." Highly vulnerable systems include the airport's underground train, airport communications boards, flight and baggage information displays, baggage handling, etc..

The airport's Century 2000 Project task force has been trying to plan for expected computer problems for more than a year.

"I think this shows an appalling lack of planning," said Michael Boyd, president of the Boyd Group, a Denver-area aviation forecasting research company. "I would have thought the one thing they could have done right at DIA was 2000 compliance. After all, the plan was to build the airport for the 21st century, " Boyd said.

If the newest, largest, most modern airport in the world is not Y2K compliant, what could we assume about thousands of other airports around the world that are not so modern — each of which may have hundreds of computer systems and thousands of embedded computer chips? Could they have even more problems than Denver International Airport?

The Bottom Line

A number of pilots have reported that they will not fly in late 1999 or early 2000. Their greatest concern is not the aircraft, but the air traffic control system. If the Airline Pilots Association is not convinced that it is safe to fly, all pilots could walk out and all U.S. aircraft would be grounded. Even if that does not occur, most travelers will postpone flying plans and take a wait-and-see attitude.

10

Where's the Beef? The Y2K Impact on Food Supplies

Food shortages, nationally and globally, could be a natural consequence of a year 2000 computer meltdown. Such shortages could result from 1) failures in the power grid; 2) banking problems that squeeze the credit lines of farmers and ranchers; 3) social unrest, which could make food deliveries into the major cities dangerous or impossible; 4) a breakdown in the railroad/truck distribution system, which is highly computer dependent and, in the case of trucking, is highly dependent on the Y2K-vulnerable Global Positioning System.

Food experts suggest we have only about 50 days of global grain reserves. Most large American cities have only four to five days of food on grocery shelves or in food warehouses, while the average family only has two to three days' supplies (or at the most a week). Many city dwellers eat in restaurants, which must be resupplied with food every two to three days. Americans are highly dependent upon various parts of the social infrastructure to provide, cook, and deliver food to us. What will they do if the year 2000 problem interrupts this finely tuned system?

Computerized Inventory Control

A primary concern in the Y2K crisis is food inventories. Most grocery stores and restaurants (fast food or otherwise) must restock every few days. Razor-thin profit margins require keeping inventories low and using a "just-in-time" (JIT) delivery mechanism to restock on a frequent basis. Much of the restocking of perishable goods takes place on a daily basis.

Inventory levels in most supermarkets are not nearly as large as a casual observer might suppose. Accelerated buying in preparation for a snowstorm or hurricane will empty most store shelves within hours. The bottom line is that precise inventory management and a well-honed delivery infrastructure are crucial for maintaining a well-stocked grocery store — a fact we tend to take for granted. A year 2000 problem can easily disrupt that delivery-inventory management process. Most large supermarkets would be lost without computerized inventory/reordering control, with date calculations essential to the whole process. They could return to manual systems, but it would take weeks or months to make such a changeover.

As Edward Yourdon wrote in *Time Bomb 2000*, "It is very possible that the inventory management systems, delivery scheduling systems, and much of the 'intelligence' that ensures the proper stockpiling of the proper items at the proper time may blow up on January 1, 2000 — indeed a few of these systems are already blowing up."

Delivery of the Food Is the Weak Link

Transporting food items from the farm, the fishery, the bakery or the slaughter house to grocery stores or restaurants may be the biggest challenge in the Y2K crisis. This requires a vast, intricate network of ships, planes, trains, and trucks — all synchronized to deliver the right amount of fresh food. The potential vulnerability of the transportation system (i.e., railroads, trucking, air traffic) to Y2K problems could "ripple" quickly into food delivery problems.

For example, a city like New York, composed of several islands and eight million people, is accessible by bridges, tunnels, boats, or planes. Massive quantities of food are shipped in each day, mostly by trucks (either owned by large companies like Dole, Heinz, etc., by dairy companies, by grocery chains or, in most cases, by independent truckers).

If America's computers go into gridlock in the first few weeks or months of the year 2000, traffic lights, bridges, and tunnels may not function properly, especially if the power grid goes down nationally or regionally, or if brownouts or blackouts occur in New York. If the banks and payments system are not functioning properly, if crime (shootings, hijackings, and robberies) increases, and if police and fire protection (without their high-tech communications) is crippled, these factors, as well, could interrupt food deliveries into the city. Under these circumstances, the supply of food moving into the cities by trucks and trains could begin to dry up, food riots could follow, and the food shortages could begin to snowball. This scenario could be played out in Washington, D.C., Boston, Newark, Atlanta, Chicago, Houston, Dallas, Miami,

Denver, Phoenix, Los Angeles, San Francisco, and dozens of other American cities.

Rural or small-town dwellers will fare much better because they are closer to the source of the food. They can barter with farmers or ranchers. They also have the capacity to be more self-sufficient and grow their own food.

Widespread food shortages in the United States and globally are likely to occur in the year 2000 as a result of the Y2K crisis. Major cities will be the hardest hit, with rural areas and small towns faring far better. Your best protection may be to not live in a major city. Secondly, you need to have a means of growing some food, of storing at least one to two years of food reserves, or both. Food reserves are likely to be very tight in the second half of 1999. Time is of the essence. If you are going to prepare for possible Y2K shortages, today is when you should begin to take action to protect your family.

11

Bureaucracies Grinding to a Halt: IRS, Social Security, Medicare

The Y2K Impact on the IRS

IRS tax systems could be unable to process returns, which in turn could jeopardize the collection of revenue and the entire tax processing system.
— "Year 2000 Computing Crisis: An Assessment Guide" (February 1997 GAO Report)

Taxpayers will be deeply grieved to know that the IRS is in trouble and may not survive the Y2K crisis — at least not in its present form. The IRS has 63–80 mainframe computers and over 100 million lines of code in 50,000 separate software programs — plus 100,000 desktop computers in their field offices. It takes one programmer about one year to fix 100,000 lines of code in COBOL language.

However, as of January 1998, the IRS had repaired only 2,000 of its 50,000 plus programs. Moreover, the IRS (with the largest civilian data-processing operation in the federal government) has only 700 programmers assigned to "fix" the 100 million lines of code. By comparison, the software inventory of the Social Security Administration (estimated at 67 million lines of code) is about two-thirds of the size of the IRS. Although the SSA utilized 400 programmers working on Y2K compliance for six years (1991–96), only six million lines of code have been corrected. The odds that the IRS will finish the repair on time are very low — zero.

Even without the Y2K crisis, the IRS has been on the brink of computer disaster for years. On January 30, 1996, the IRS admitted publicly that its 11-year, $4-billion computer upgrade had failed. The IRS' assistant commissioner, Arthur Gross, (who recently resigned as head of the IRS' Y2K compliance program) told a commission established by Congress that the agency's systems are "dysfunctional." "Nevertheless," he said, "the IRS must continue to use these systems for the foreseeable future," (*New York Times*, January 31, 1996).

On February 5, 1996, the *Wall Street Journal* published an editorial written by Shelly Davis, former IRS historian. Commenting on the year 2000 problem, she wrote, "Without decisive congressional action there may only be a few years before we face an IRS meltdown. The looming 'year 2000' software conversion issue brings a chill to those who realize its seriousness. The same Arthur Gross who admitted the intellectual lapses of the IRS, said last fall that a failure to complete this conversion 'would mean a major disabling of the IRS.'"

The day after the publication of this article, Dr. Gary North interviewed Ms. Davis and asked her if the IRS would be flying blind if the revision of its code turns out to be as big a failure as the last 11 years worth of revisions. She said that "flying blind" describes it perfectly. Then she made an amazing statement: the figure of 11 years is an underestimate. She said that the IRS has been trying to update its computers for 30 years. Each time, the update has failed. She said that by renaming each successive attempt, the IRS has concealed a problem that has been going on for 30 years.

As if the IRS' computer/Y2K problems were not bad enough, they actually may not have until December 31, 1999 to fix the problem. The government's computers will actually roll over to the year 2000 early, on July 1, 1999, because they are based on fiscal year calculations. Internal Revenue Service Y2K problems could actually begin on July 1, 1999 and escalate into the year 2000.

As the general public begins to become aware of the IRS' major (possibly terminal) collection and processing problems, tax noncompliance could grow from a trickle to a flood by early year 2000. For that reason Ed Yardeni, Michael Higgins, a number of Y2K consultants, and a growing chorus of voices in Congress are calling for abolition (or major restructuring) of the IRS and a move to a flat tax or consumption tax by the turn of the century. The potential for a precipitous decline in tax receipts in the year 2000 is making many government officials, in and out of Congress, very nervous indeed.

The Y2K Impact on Social Security

The Social Security Administration (SSA) mails out 50 million checks per month. If their Y2K fix is 99.6 percent accurate, which is highly unlikely (a 0.4% error rate), 200,000 checks will still be mailed out monthly with faulty information. This logistics nightmare could cause a system-wide gridlock at the agency.

It is hard to imagine a more date-sensitive government agency than the SSA. When were you born? When did you begin working? How much FICA contribution did you make in each of your income-generating years? When did you stop working? When did you begin drawing Social Security payments? All of this information requires dates and date-related arithmetic. Dates and date arithmetic are embedded in a Y2K-compromised system, now estimated to contain 67 million lines of code. To fix its computer systems, the SSA needs to hire 11,000 additional COBOL programmers in 1998 to be compliant by 2000, but there are not that many available COBOL programmers in the whole world.

In mid-1997, the SSA obtained a number of new computer programs and new programmers. They announced they would be compliant by 2000. However, shortly thereafter, SSA discovered an additional 33 million lines of code in 54 state-administered Social Security programs covering 12 million individuals.

The discovery of 33 million additional lines of code is very problematic for SSA. They now have a multi-front battle. Instead of one big repair job on their Washington computers, they must now dispatch their technicians to 50 separate states.

In his book, *Time Bomb 2000*, Edward Yourdon warns

about the "systemic" problems SSA faces, even if they should miraculously become Y2K compliant:

> Many of the checks produced by SSA and other government agencies are now deposited directly into the recipient's bank, rather than being printed out and mailed through the postal system.
>
> This means that there are at least two computer systems within SSA (one that was developed originally for computing and printing retirement checks, and a newer one to siphon off a subset of those payments and transmit them to the bank, via magnetic tape or telecommunications link), plus at least one computer system within the banks to process the incoming payments and funnel them into the proper account, plus one or more computer systems that support the "inter-bank" financial transfers between all manner of financial institutions.
>
> Thus, even if SSA does its job correctly, there's no guarantee that a retired widow will find that her monthly check has landed in the right account at the right time.

What is ominous about the present Y2K repair program in the SSA is that that agency was thought to be much further ahead than any other government agency. As these groups (and tens of thousands of businesses across America) move into the Y2K repair process, they are finding many more problems and hurdles than they first anticipated. The problem keeps on growing.

The Y2K Impact on Medicare

Thirty-eight million Americans are covered by Medicare, which paid out $288 million in claims in 1997. In the year 2000, Medicare is expected to process one billion claims. In a May 1997 report entitled "Medicare Transaction System: Success Depends Upon Correcting Critical Managerial and Technical Weaknesses," the General Accounting Office (GAO) warned of a looming crisis in the Medicare system. They concluded that there is no evidence to suggest that Medicare will make the year 2000 deadline.

The Medicare system is administered by 70 private firms whose computers must all interface together and whose network must also communicate with the nation's thousands of medical facilities, medical hardware companies, pharmaceutical providers, insurance agencies, banks, etc. If any main link or group of small links in this network malfunctioned, the whole system could falter.

The Health Care Financing Administration (HCFA) is charged with overseeing the Y2K compliance of the 70 firms, but the GAO report also accused HCFA of not overseeing the task properly or having a contingency plan if Medicare is not compliant by 2000:

> Unless timely, effective systems changes are implemented as the year 2000 approaches, HCFA may be unable to process claims accurately and within required time frames. The potential risks associated with not being ready for 2000 are serious, since virtually all Medicare transactions depend, to some degree, on dates to determine benefits eligibility — dates of birth, medical procedure, other insurance coverage, and so forth.

The danger is that, if not corrected, systems could well read the computer-coded "oo" as 1900, not 2000. All date-dependent calculations would therefore be affected, having an obvious impact on age and beneficiary claims.

These federal agencies are not the only government agencies in trouble. The Office of Management and Budget (OMB) and congressional committies have been assessing the progress of Y2K compliance in the various agencies of the federal government. What they have discovered is alarming.

The U.S. Government Office of Management and Budget's Fourth Quarter 1997 survey of government agency compliance indicated that 10 of 24 agencies are critically behind in upgrading their systems. The 14 agencies that are supposedly making headway cannot substantiate or document their progress.

Below is a list of U.S. departments and agencies and the percentage of Y2K compliance they have achieved as of September 9, 1998, according to the Koenig Y2K Report Card, which is based on the federal government's Y2K status report.

Source: U.S. Federal Government's Quarterly Report on Y2K Readiness.

Agriculture Department	50 Percent
Commerce Department (includes Patent and Trademark Office)	59 percent
Defense Department	27 percent
Education Department (includes Sandia National Laboratory)	13 percent
Health and Human Services (includes Medicaid, Medicare)	14 percent

Housing and Urban Development	40 percent
Justice Department (includes FBI)	18 percent
Labor Department	19 percent
State Department	0 percent
Transportation Department (includes FAA)	11 percent
Treasury Department (includes IRS, BATF)	44 percent
Federal Emergency Management Agency	47 percent
NASA	51 percent
Social Security Administration	87 percent

The Office of Management and Budget has estimated the following compliance dates for certain key government departments or agencies:

Agency	Estimated date of Y2K compliance
Department of Labor & Energy	2019
Department of Defense	2012
Department of Transportation (including FAA)	2010
Department of Agriculture	2005
Department of Treasury (including IRS)	2004
General Services Administration (GSA)	2002
Department of Justice	2001
Federal Emergency Management Agency (FEMA)	2000.5

It is alarming to know that (according to the OMB Report) the agency responsible for bailing us out of disasters (FEMA) and implementing a state of national emergency won't be ready to respond to the effects of the Y2K crisis until the second half of the year 2000.

Conclusion: The U.S. federal government is hopelessly behind in Y2K remediation — receiving somewhere between a "D" and an "F" from Rep. Horn. Each time the grades come out, they're worse than before. As Rep. Horn recently said, "The executive branch is . . . on the edge of failure. (They have) almost 8,000 mission-critical computer systems . . . At the current rate of progress, only 63 percent of these systems will be ready for the date change . . . We have a long way to go and a short time to get there."

According to Horn's congressional committee, 15 of the 24 largest departments and agencies will not complete repairs to their mission-critical systems in time for the January 1, 2000 deadline. Over 3,000 critical government services will not be working after December 31, 1999. Government-wide, more than one-third of mission-critical computer systems will not be repaired in time.

The Justice Department (including the FBI) and the Health and Human Services Department (including Medicare and Medicaid) won't be ready until 2001; the U.S. Treasury (including the IRS) not until 2004; the Agriculture Department (including food stamps and farm subsidies) not until 2005; the Department of Transportation (including the FAA and air traffic control system) not until 2010; the Department of Defense, not until 2012; the State Department (get your passports updated now), not until 2019.

In summary, the federal government is in a severe Y2K crisis with very little hope of recovery. Their inventory of computer systems is gargantuan. The lion's share of their software is very old, and for the most part, written in obscure computer languages for which there are few programmers. The government's organizational inefficiency is widely recognized. They do an especially bad job managing crises when under time constraints.

Jim Lord, who worked in a high-tech capacity for the government for 38 years, gave the following analysis:

> Their technical staff and contract administrators are marginally competent, poorly motivated, and badly managed. Most importantly, the government's top leadership in the major departments and in the White House is not technically astute, is inadequately advised, and has not accepted Y2K as a survival issue. OMB's quarterly reports are a sham with no reporting on millions of "Y2K impaired" personal computers, embedded systems, or the "Domino Effec" of Y2K.

> The bottom line is, a) only 14 percent of all large software projects are finished on schedule, b) this project has an inflexible deadline, c) Y2K is the largest software project in history, and d) government owns the biggest share of the problem.

The U.S. government is hopelessly behind on the Y2K crisis, which could bring the government to its knees after January 1, 2000. Don't look for the government to come in and save the rest of the system; they need to save themselves. At a time when we need a "Manhattan Project" or "Man on the Moon"-type national effort, we are instead getting apathy, disorganization, confusion, sugar coating (i.e., misinformation), and "cover our backside"-type responses from most of the bureaucracy, from President Clinton on down.

12

The Impact of the Y2K Crisis on National Defense

> The Year 2000 work that the DOD [Department of Defense] faces will be by far the largest and most difficult project it has ever undertaken. Frankly, we think the odds of it finishing all of its work on time are zero.
>
> — Edward Yourdon, *Time Bomb 2000*

The U.S. military is the most computerized of all U.S. government agencies and the most computerized and software-intensive military in the world. It actually began the computer revolution during World War II, and is believed to have more computers and software than all the other armed forces in the world combined. It is estimated that the Department of Defense (DOD) has six million separate software applications, 1,000 software sites, and 300 million software function points (30 billion COBOL program instructions) that require 200,000 software professionals in and out of the military to run the system.

In addition, there are millions of computer chips embedded in military weapons, for which the consequences of a year 2000 software bug could be catastrophic. Planes, missiles, bombs, tanks, satellites, ships, air defense systems, and devices whose existence DOD has never admitted in public are controlled by or interact with date-sensitive computer chips.

In addition, it is estimated that 70–90 percent of the U.S. military's computers must be corrected to meet Y2K compliance. According to *Information Week* (February 19, 1997), the DOD claimed in early 1997 that it had 7800 computer systems (each consisting of many individual computers), of which only 302 were Y2K compliant. Seven months later in September 1997, DOD admitted that it had 13,897 computer systems and that none of them were Y2K compliant.

On May 10, 1998, the *Rocky Mountain News* reported that as of February 1998, only 18.3 percent of the military's mission-critical computer systems were prepared for the year 2000.

John Pike, an analyst with the Federation of American Scientists, a think tank based in Washington D.C., says that U.S. strategic nuclear systems should be easier than other Defense Department computers to debug because they are closed off from other computer systems for security reasons. Once cleared of the bug, they cannot be easily reinfected. That does not lessen his concern.

"It's sort of like Caesar's wife," Pike said. The strategic forces have "got the biggest burden of anybody in terms of publicly demonstrating that they're year 2000-compliant. That's got to be one where the margin for error, the fault tolerance, should be pretty close to zero. If FAA fouls up, some 747s crash. If STRATCOM fouls up, they incinerate the northern hemisphere."

"It is a great steaming heap of spaghetti code — which means that it works but nobody knows why anymore," Pike said. "And nobody wants to look too closely for fear that they might break it. When they go in there to start looking at this code, it turns out that half the code doesn't even execute anymore.

"Which would basically be your car having a dozen cylinders instead of six and only six work and you have no idea which six. And no one can explain to you why this seems to be the case."

According to Rep. Steven Horn, the U.S. military has 358 million lines of computer code to correct; other estimates range between one and two billion lines. The problem is that the DOD's computers use many ancient computer languages that are far more obscure than COBOL and unknown to most modern programmers — languages such as Jovial, CS-1, CMS-2, TACPoL, NELIAC. No one programs in these languages anymore.

At a press conference on December 12, 1997, Rep. Horn said that the U.S. military will require 21 years to fix just their mission-critical computers. On January 1, 2000, America's military computers and embedded chips are going down. These systems are not Y2K compliant. The U.S. military has massively downsized over the past five to ten years, while becoming almost totally dependent on high-tech weapons and fighting capabilities, as was amply demonstrated in the Desert Storm War in 1990.

The Defense Department Is in Trouble

When Ed Yardeni and John Koskinen were interviewed by CNN about Y2K on July 18, 1998, they both concurred that the number-one Y2K problem that America faces is its noncompliant Department of Defense. By January 1, 2000, it is estimated that the Defense Department is likely to have only about one-third of its mission-critical systems Y2K compliant. With the world's largest payroll and an arsenal of air, land, and sea weapons dependent on computers, the Pentagon (which will spend over $10 billion over the next 18 months on Y2K remediation efforts) is hopelessly behind. The DOD did not even become fully aware of the Y2K problem until 1995! Rep. Horn's committee projects that the Defense Department cannot be compliant until 2012.

DOD Y2K Remediation Is a Moving Target

No one knows (not even Congressional investigators) how many computer systems the military has to correct — the number is a moving target. In the third quarter of 1997, the DOD reported that it had 25,054 affected systems, 3,143 of which were identified as "mission critical." Of these, only 672 systems were "said to be" compliant (but not proven so), 203 are being replaced, 128 are being terminated, 2,140 need to be reprogrammed, and 148 were in assessment. Not surprisingly, only 37 had been fixed.

It is important to note that bureaucrats in the DOD and other government agencies often play games with the term "mission critical." If they understate what is "mission critical," they make their remediation efforts and the condition of their department or agency look better than it really is.

On June 12, 1998, Rep. Steven Horn's Y2K committee revealed that the DOD had falsified the number of systems that were compliant. The Pentagon's inspector general found that the DOD had greatly exaggerated how many systems had been repaired.

That same day the *Washington Post* reported on the scandal:

> "Senior DOD management cannot afford to make Y2K program decisions based on highly inaccurate information," the office of the inspector general concluded in its report on the matter. "If DOD does not take the action that it needs to obtain accurate information as to the status of its Y2K efforts, we believe that serious Y2K failures may occur in DOD mission-critical information technology systems."

> Rep. Stephen Horn (R-CA) raised the report at a House subcommittee hearing Wednesday on Year 2000 computer repairs. "I thought we were past the days of the Vietnam body count," Horn said as he inquired about Pentagon plans for improved honesty of compliance. The department has about 25,000 computer systems, with about 2,800 designated as "mission critical."

> They include command and control, satellite, inventory management, transportation management, medical and equipment, plus pay and personnel systems.

> But when the office of the inspector general sampled 430 computer systems that the Pentagon had reported as year 2000 compliant in November 1997, it found that defense officials could not

provide documents to show they had followed proper procedures. Using a statistical model, the office concluded "that between 265 and 338 systems were not certified," although the systems had been reported to senior management as certified.

In addition, investigators found that "the existence of a completed and signed Y2K compliance checklist did not always mean that the system was Y2K compliant."

The report, issued last month, underscores the problems that federal agencies face as they try to define such terms as "Y2K compliant" and "Y2K ready."

The Agriculture Department, for example, recently reported 15 systems as compliant, even though they were only in developmental stages, said Joel C. Willemssen of the General Accounting Office.

"The word 'certified' had so many different kinds of meanings that it had lost all its meaning," Brown said yesterday.

The Implications of Having Only One-third of Our Mission-Critical Defense Systems Working in 2000

Computer consultant Jim Lord analyzed this problem in his *Year 2000 Survival Newsletter* (March 3, 1998):

The Defense Department recently received a letter grade of "F" and is projected to have only one-third of its essential computing systems working properly by the year 2000. This is nothing less than scandalous. DOD has about 25,000 computing systems, of which 2,915 have been identified as "mission critical."

It is vital to understand the term "mission-critical system." Think back to the Gulf War against Iraq eight years ago. One of my own unforgettable memories of that event was the incredible television images of Tomahawk missiles fired by ships far out at sea.

This writer can still see those missiles flying low over the cameras on the way to their targets inland. (They had a very special, personal significance to me because my son, a U.S. Marine, was on the ground in Saudi Arabia. In my mind's eye, every one of those missiles was on its way to protecting his life.)

There are thousands of identical Tomahawk missiles but only a single Tomahawk Missile System. This system is designed to accomplish a specific mission that is critical to the objectives of the military. In this case, the mission might be to "destroy land-based targets with missiles fired from surface ships, submarines or aircraft from a distance of 1,000 miles," for example.

Each Tomahawk missile has embedded computers that use identical software. If this software has a year 2000 defect, the software engineers must correct the problem only once and then replace the bad software in each missile. If this step is not taken, of course, the military would lose the capability to perform the specified mission because thousands of missiles would be rendered useless by the mal-functioning software.

When it is reported that Y2K repairs to a mission-critical system will not be completed by the dead-line, it means that all individual copies of that system will become defective and the fundamental mission capability will be lost or impaired. In the case of the Tomahawk, thousands of individual missiles would become inoperative and the mili-tary would no longer be able to destroy land-based targets with missiles from 1,000 miles away.

The Horn Report Card projects that nearly 3,000 mission critical systems throughout the govern-ment will not be ready for the year 2000. Nearly 1,800 of these are military systems. This is, of course, a catastrophic loss of military capability that would likely render the American military a helpless giant.

The GAO Issues an Ominous Report on the DOD's Y2K Non-preparedness

Following are excerpts from an article in the *Rocky Moun-tain News* (May 10, 1998) entitled "The Y2K Bug: As Time Runs Short, Strategic Defense Computers in Colorado Springs Not Ready to Handle Year 2000 Glitch":

Authorities are investigating whether the nation's strategic defense computers could malfunction be-cause of the "millennium bug." "Some military computers are almost certain to fail after the clock strikes midnight on Dec. 31, 1999," said John Stephenson, who heads the study by the General

Accounting Office, the investigative arm of Congress.

In an April 30th report to Congress, the GAO warned that "time is running out" to protect the military's 1.5 million computers. "What you hope is that (defense officials) will start to apply triage," Stephenson told the *Rocky Mountain News*. "They should decide what their most important missions are and which systems support those missions and fix those first." A top GAO priority is the North American Aerospace Defense Command in Colorado Springs, a facility that monitors America's nuclear defenses. The installation at Cheyenne Mountain is the linchpin of strategic forces. Its computer-powered equipment can detect incoming enemy missiles. The GAO also may review the satellite relay stations at Buckley Air National Guard Base in Aurora. Those facilities track missile firings and nuclear explosions.

"We are looking at NORAD in terms of the integrated tactical attack assessment system," said Yvonne Vigil, an evaluator in the Denver region GAO office. Describing the complicated NORAD facility as the "system of all systems," Vigil said NORAD's computers must be bug-free because their mission is "to protect and safeguard the United States."

Perhaps the most critical area is the military, in which many old systems — called "legacy systems" — still play major roles. The software coding is so archaic that finding the sections calculating dates is difficult. A congressional committee estimated in 1996 that the Department of Defense must examine 358 million lines of code to fix Y2K problems.

Already, a test has shown that the Department of Defense's Global Command Control System failed when the clock was pushed ahead to the year 2000. Deployed at 700 military installations worldwide, the system is the key tool in battle management and planning. Other vulnerable systems include the Global Positioning System used for determining a military unit's exact location and for the precision targeting of "smart" weapons.

Other military communications systems could be compromised. Even on-board computers in jet fighters will be tested, the GAO report said. The report slammed the Department of Defense's handling of the millennium bug problem. The Pentagon did not have a complete inventory of its computers, was wasting too much time trying to fix noncritical systems and had inadequate contingency plans if important systems crash, the report said.

"They've designated 2,900 mission-critical systems and 25,000 nonmission-critical systems," Stephenson told the *News*. "But if you look at the statistics, (the systems) are being repaired at about the same rate. So what's the point of designating "mission critical" if it doesn't mean you focus your resources and priority on those?

"The more they get into assessment of this, they're

finding it's more insidious than first thought," the GAO's Stephenson said. The GAO reports over the past two years on the military's 2000 problem have steadily increased in their alarm. In the April report, the GAO warned bluntly that failing to quickly fix the problem would mean computer failures that are "widespread, costly and potentially disruptive to military operations worldwide.

"All the federal government reports that we do will ratchet up without trying to create panic," Stephenson said. "We're becoming increasingly concerned. Some of the big private-sector institutions like banks are ahead of the federal government," he said. "They provide a good benchmark for the federal government and they're showing that testing is much more difficult and takes a lot longer than originally anticipated."

"The Department of Defense is peculiarly vulnerable to this problem because it has such a grotesque set of legacy (older) systems," Stephenson said. "It has an awful lot of systems that have been around for an awfully long time." Though computer systems at NORAD's Cheyenne Mountain installation are being upgraded, some military machines still calculate dates in archaic computer programming languages that are no longer in use. Many programmers who wrote the code have retired or adapted to more modern computer languages.

Reviewing tens of millions of lines of military code to find the exact coding for dates and time is intensely time-consuming.

GAO Says That the Millennium Bug Threatens U.S. Naval Operations

The *Orange County Register* (July 1, 1998) reported the following:

> U.S. Navy operations worldwide could be severely disrupted by any failure to fix the Year 2000 computer bug in critical systems, the audit and investigations arm of Congress said Tuesday.
>
> "Failure to address the Year 2000 problem in time could severely degrade or disrupt the Navy's day-to-day and, more importantly, mission-critical operations," the General Accounting Office said.
>
> The GAO said the glitch could disrupt everything from navy combat capabilities to communications, intelligence gathering, surveillance and fleet mobilization and readiness. In a report requested by lawmakers, the GAO said the Navy was behind schedule in fixing the problem.
>
> In a reply included with the report, the Navy agreed to a GAO recommendation that it establish a complete and accurate inventory of information systems and to plan for the continuity of all its critical military operations and business processes rather than only a part of "mission-critical" systems.

Secretary of the Navy John H. Dalton has called for the full involvement of U.S. naval leadership in Y2K issues. He has said the United States cannot afford to approach the problem with a business-as-usual attitude. The problem touches virtually all areas of the Navy and Marine

Corps from foxholes, to flight lines, to destroyer deck-plates as well as shore infrastructure.

The DOD Is Demoted on OMB's Y2K Preparedness List

The Department of Defense, Veterans Affairs, and Interior have slowed in their efforts to fix their year 2000 problems in the past three months, according to the Office of Management and Budget (OMB). A recent report by the OMB outlines progress of 24 federal agencies in fixing their year 2000 problems for the quarter ending May 15, 1998. The DOD dropped in the OMB's ranking from Tier II (agencies that show evidence of progress but are still a concern) to Tier I, OMB's "critical tier," meaning that OMB has assessed that there is "insufficient evidence of adequate progress" in fixing year 2000 problems. The Veterans' Administration and Department of Interior both fell from Tier III (the highest ranking) to Tier II.

U.S. Air Defenses Could Be Crippled by Y2K

What if Russia, China, or a radical Islamic state launched nuclear missiles at America at a time when NORAD (North American Air Defense) computers were down due to Y2K? Can those computers go down? Would we be blind to such an attack until shortly before impact? On June 21, 1998, Fred Kaplan of the *Boston Globe* reported on a military test that failed:

> New York: Sometime in 1993 — memories are hazy and nothing was written down for the public — the North American Air Defense Command in Cheyenne Mountain, Colo., conducted a test to see what would happen to all their computers — the ones

that warn of a nuclear attack — on New Year's day of the Year 2000.

As with nearly all computers, years were designated only by their last two digits — '98' for 1998, '99' for 1999, and so on. A few engineers were starting to speculate: When 2000 comes along, the computers would read it as '00' and think it was 1900. What would happen?

What happened was, everything froze — the screens that monitored the early-warning satellites and radars and other communications systems that would detect a flock of missiles or bombers coming our way. "It all locked up at the stroke of midnight," recalled Robert Martin, a top computer specialist.

Martin was not present at the simulation, but his life has been ruled by it ever since. At the Mitre Corp. in Bedford, one of the leading Pentagon contractors working to solve this problem, Martin is the "focal point" for "Y2K."

The problem is hardly restricted to NORAD. The Defense Department has about 25,000 computer systems — 2,803 of them classified as "mission-critical systems," meaning that, without them, the military could no longer carry out a major mission.

"These include computers for 'all kinds' of weapons," Martin said, "'the full spectrum' from nuclear missiles to a sergeant's battlefield laptop, as well as the various satellites, sensors, radars, and communications networks that link them into a unified fighting machine."

Asked what computers are not affected by the Year 2000 problem, Martin replied, "I can't think of many."

Recently an undisclosed DOD source indicated that the DOD had been trying to run simulated programs on nuclear missile silo computers to see what would happen on January 1, 2000. In short, there was a total breakdown of the fail-safe protection. Some missiles shut down totally. Others fired their missiles without orders. Other DOD sources have reported that missiles in silos armed with nuclear warheads may self-destruct in the silo.

The USS Yorktown is the U.S. Navy's showcase "Smartship." This cruiser was outfitted with a $10 million super-accurate satellite guidance and fiber-optic computer network designed to make navigation and electronic warfare a fingertip affair. *USA Today* (September 26, 1997), in an article entitled "Computer Blip Teaches 'Smartship' a Lesson" reported the following:

> The Navy's new high-tech wonder sat dead in the water off the Virginia coast last weekend as sailors discovered that high-tech computers don't always work . . . Touch the map on a color screen, confirm, and that's where the ship goes. Sensors monitor heat and vibrations that might signal an impending failure of a motor or pump. Supposedly. But success hinges on a computer. And in the wee hours last Saturday it went down. The Navy won't say exactly what went wrong, except that a bug showed up in the software.

Concern at the CIA About Y2K Threats to U.S. Security

In a *USA Today* (June 25, 1998) article entitled "Year 2000 Bug Poses Security Risk, CIA Warns," CIA director George Tenet warned that the year 2000 problem could help adversaries penetrate critical U.S. business, government, and defense computers:

> "We are building an information infrastructure, the most complex the world has ever known, on an insecure foundation," he said . . .

> Tenet's testimony before the Senate Governmental Affairs Committee added a new layer to those worries. Because companies and the government must open their systems to repair, the so-called Y2K (for Year 2000) bug "provides all kinds of opportunities for someone with hostile intent" to gain information — or plant viruses, he said. One CIA concern: Many of the programmers working on the problem are non-Americans and the programs are foreign-produced. If bugs are implanted or programs stolen, "it's something you may not know about for many years," Tenet said.

> And even if the repairs are secure, Tenet said hackers or foreign enemies may enter U.S. computers unnoticed, because people will blame evidence of their attacks on Y2K problems.

> "So far, most attacks on information systems are from hackers. But there is at least one intrusion effort that might be sponsored by a hostile state," Tenet said. Those incidents may increase as computer technology spreads around the world.

Overall, Tenet said the United States was ahead of other countries in dealing with computer terrorism and the Y2K bug. On the other hand, he said, "the United States is the biggest target and defense against cyberattack is still in its infancy."

Y2K Espionage Potential

The United States is hustling to find computer programmers to fix the Y2K problem. We have changed our immigration laws to allow 90,000 computer programmers to immigrate to this country this year. There is serious concern that in the press to fix our systems nationwide, foreign spies could make off with information while they're working on Y2K programming. They could also add bugs, viruses, or snooping capability to programs. The need for sufficient oversight is a concern.

Cyberattacks Are More Likely Due to Y2K

The Center for Infrastructural Warfare Studies Assessment is concerned about computer-attack vulnerabilities that would "wrap around" the Y2K crisis. Of particular concern are "referenced attacks." This term refers to an attack that begins when computer operators respond to a perceived threat. When they reboot their computers in response to the threat, stage 2 of the attack occurs because the rebooting process enables the real virus to activate and cause significant damage to the system. The Center is currently concerned about the vulnerability of the U.S. financial system.

The *Los Angeles Times* (May 4, 1998), in an article entitled "Do Computers Pose Nuclear Threat," reported the following:

Over the last three weeks, a new group of computer hackers that calls itself Masters of Downloading has released information to back up its claim to have penetrated sensitive Pentagon computer systems.

The group claims to have stolen software of the Defense Information Systems Network Equipment Manager, which controls military communications systems, including global-positioning satellites. The group of 15 hackers, which includes two from Russia, released a statement and a sample of the software, complete with interface screens.

The "masters" also announced that they had cracked communications links to U.S. submarines. The Defense Department says it is treating the group's intrusion "very seriously," but it downplayed the significance of the break-ins.

A test attack by a team of military hackers has proved that they can cripple the U.S. military and the U.S. power grid by using hacking programs available on the Internet. Both the U.S. military and the power grid are completely vulnerable. The *Washington Times* (April 16, 1998) described the operation:

> Senior Pentagon leaders were stunned by a military exercise showing how easy it is for hackers to cripple U.S. military and civilian computer networks, according to new details of the secret exercise.
>
> Using software obtained easily from hacker sites on the Internet, a group of National Security Agency

officials could have shut down the U.S. electric-power grid within days and rendered impotent the command-and-control elements of the U.S. Pacific Command, said officials familiar with the war game, known as Eligible Receiver.

"The attack was actually run in a two-week period and the results were frightening," said a defense official involved in the game.

"This attack, run by a set of people using standard Internet techniques, would have basically shut down the command-and-control capability in the Pacific theater for some considerable period of time."

The secret exercise began last June after months of preparation by the NSA computer specialists who, without warning, targeted computers used by U.S. military forces in the Pacific and in the United States.

The game was simple: Conduct information warfare attacks, or "inforwar," on the Pacific Command and ultimately force the United States to soften its policies toward the crumbling Communist regime in Pyongyang. The "hackers" posed as paid surrogates for North Korea.

According to U.S. officials who took part in the exercise, within days the team of 50 to 75 NSA officials had inflicted crippling damage. They broke into computer networks and gained access to the systems that control the electrical power grid for the entire country. If they had wanted to, the hackers could have disabled the grid, leaving the United States in the dark.

Groups of NSA hackers based in Hawaii and other parts of the United States floated effortlessly through global cyberspace, breaking into unclassified military computer networks in Hawaii, the headquarters of the U.S. Pacific Command, as well as in Washington, Chicago, St. Louis, and parts of Colorado.

"The attacks were not actually run against the infrastructure components because we don't want to do things like shut down the power grid," said a defense official involved in the exercise. "But the referees were shown the attacks and shown the structure of the power-grid control, and they agreed, yeah, this attack would have shut down the power grid."

The attackers also foiled virtually all efforts to trace them. FBI agents joined the Pentagon in trying to find the hackers, but for the most part they failed. Only one of the several NSA groups, a unit based in the United States, was uncovered. The rest operated without being located or identified.

What if these hackers had been working for the militaries or intelligence services of Russia, China, North Korea or some radical Islamic state like Iraq, Iran, Syria, Libya, or some terrorist group that hates America? Could they do it? This operation proves that they could. Would they do it? Will they do it? In the crisis and confusion that Y2K is guaranteed to generate, we are very vulnerable. Though for the test operations purpose, the NSA team targeted only the Pacific Command, it is clear that they could have targeted almost any command in the U.S. military. If they could bring down the U.S. power grid, could they have brought down Wall Street or the U.S. banking system?

Not all computer hackers are bored computer nerds, simply "tweaking" the system for entertainment or laughs. Some work for the Chinese Communist and Russian intelligence services (in the latter case, the KGB and GRU [Military Intelligence], which are still very much in existence and as strong as during the Cold War). Others work for radical Islamic governments that hate America and that are themselves in possession of nuclear, biological, and chemical weapons.

There are several Y2K-related nuclear launch scenarios that are troubling Pentagon officials at present.

1) Late 1999 or early 2000 would be an excellent time to launch a nuclear attack while the enemy (America) is blind, can't rely on the data it is receiving, and doesn't know whether to respond.

2) How will nations react when their early warning screens go blank and they can't tell whether a missile attack has been launched against them?

3) What if hackers penetrate NORAD or our strategic missile forces and either scramble data, give false data that would indicate we are under attack, or create data that says we are not under attack when, in fact, we are?

4) Would Russia or China use this Y2K period of confusion in U.S. strategic defense and missile systems to launch an attack against the U.S.?

At present, Russia (and its military) seems to be woefully behind in its Y2K remediations, with no apparent sense of urgency to get the repairs done. Is this real or is this misinformation? On the other hand, if Russia's nuclear forces are in the state of disarray that many people believe, with nukes not properly maintained, and its early warning system in disrepair, could this lead to a nuclear incident, an accidental launch?

Quoting Bruce Blair, the *Los Angeles Times* (May 4, 1998) reported the following:

> Into this dark picture we can insert computer unreliability, such as the year 2000 problem — which Blair says the Russians haven't begun to solve — and confusing and conflicting information scrambled or manipulated by anonymous hackers. While it is probably impossible for hackers to get into systems that might enable an unauthorized launch of nuclear weapons — although even this is not completely certain — the growing number of penetrations of Pentagon systems raises the specter of unreliability and confusion in a crisis. Computer data may not be the trigger on a nuclear warhead, but it could lead someone to pull that trigger hastily.

America's Global Positioning System Is at Risk

The following analysis of America's GPS, its Y2K vulnerability, and the implications of same was written by an individual, who wishes to remain anonymous, who works closely with America's largest defense and aerospace contractor and the DOD:

> On the surface, many people think they are thoroughly familiar with the Global Positioning System (GPS) of 24 Navstar satellites. Most commonly understand that it is used to determine an

individual's location in relation to the surface of the earth. The Navy uses the system to enable its ships and submarines to track their own position with great accuracy. The Army and Marine Corps use GPS to enable their ground troops to accurately track their positions on the battlefield. The Air Force uses GPS to allow their planes to keep a running fix on their current position so that they do not fly into someone's airspace accidentally and start a war. All of this is common knowledge.

"DOD plans for all military aircraft to use GPS for navigation by 2000 and the military's growing dependence on GPS-guided smart bombs have heightened Pentagon concerns about the vulnerability of the navigation system to year 2000 glitches (not to mention rollover on August 22, 1999)," (*Government Computer News* [April 14, 1997]).

What many are not so aware of, however, is another, absolutely critical function of the GPS satellites. The computers on board these satellites rely on highly accurate atomic clocks (more accurate than any clock on earth other than the Primary Standards Clocks in Washington) to send down precise navigational signals for receivers to plot their positions from. For instance, the military relies on GPS to enable their missile systems from ICBMs to Patriot anti-missile defense systems to find their targets.

As the *Government Computer News* (April 14, 1997) said, "First showcased during Operation Desert

Storm, GPS has become the source for precise and accurate targeting information for the Tomahawk cruise missile, Joint Direct Attack Munition, Army Tactical Missile System, and Joint Standoff Weapon."

The military and private industry have found other uses for these clocks, however. The Defense Communication Agency (renamed Defense Information System Agency [DISA] in 1991) in the late '80s and early '90s upgraded their communication system from the older LORAN-C models to GPS synchronized networks capable of moving sizeable amounts of data and voice communications with great accuracy. This system is essential to allowing timely transfer of information and voice data anywhere in the world where U.S. forces are stationed. This can be on a ship, deep inside a missile silo, or on the ground in the middle of a pitched battle. Without this system, the military will find it nearly impossible to coordinate large-scale battle plans.

The DCS (Defense Communication System) communication system is tremendously efficient because it is able to function in a synchronized fashion, thereby allowing all parts of the network to function as if it were one. The highly touted Global Command and Control System (GCCS) uses this network to send and receive data from military units all over the world. This is the Achilles' heel of the military. The entire network relies upon the hyper-accurate clocks within the GPS satellites to synchronize U.S. military data transmission planet-wide.

Without the GPS clocks to keep the networks synchronized, the system crashes, worldwide.

The banking system of the western world is entirely interconnected. This interconnectivity is necessary because banks need up-to-date information on everything from currency exchange rates (which can change from minute to minute), interest rates from various central banks, and wiring trillions of dollars around the world daily. This system is an extremely high-tech venture, utilizing the latest in synchronized digital networks. These networks rely upon GPS as well, and if anything happens to the synchronization feeds from the GPS, the network will crash, with millions, perhaps billions of dollars being "lost" both to data corruption, and to lost business every single day it stays down. It is estimated by banking experts that if the system were to go down for a full week, there would be a worldwide global depression that would last at least a decade.

On August 22, 1999, the GPS satellite system's clocks will roll back 1024 weeks, making global network synchronization impossible.

The effects of this failure cannot be overstated. While the majority of the world is focusing on Y2K, the GPS vulnerability is quietly being overlooked, with extremely grave implications. The banking system alone may never recover, with its interconnectivity, which in one sense is its life blood. With this interconnectivity severed, their only hope for survival is to go back to a paper system, which is patently impossible. The projections above of the global impact of a one-week shutdown are frighteningly optimistic given that the Boeing Company, currently upgrading GPS to deal with the date rollover problem, says that it will complete its task, at the earliest, in December of 1999, a full four months after rollover is scheduled to occur (on August 22, 1999).

The Russian leaders want in the worst way to become a dominant world power once again. They know that if they do not act soon, the infrastructure (electricity, and utilities such as water and sewer that run off electricity) they inherited from the former Soviet Empire will fail from Y2K-related issues, and their situation will be even more desperate. They know that they will never be the world power that they were until the U.S. and its allies in NATO are gone, and a window of opportunity for doing just that is opening that has never occurred since World War II.

The cold war between the two super powers was basically a stalemate, founded on the principle of MAD (Mutually Assured Destruction). If one side launched, the other would launch back and both sides would be destroyed. This "balance of power" has been maintained for 50 years. That, however, is about to change.

It is widely reported that the U.S. arsenal of nuclear ICBMs utilizes GPS to guide themselves to their targets. This is by far the most accurate method of targeting yet invented. It is, however, going to malfunction on August 22, 1999, when the GPS system rolls back and begins to produce erroneous navigational data.

"In April 1996 the DOD awarded Boeing Company the $1.3 billion GPS block IIF satellite contract to correct the imminent GPS rollover problem. It is replacing existing flawed equipment with the IMOSC (Integrated Mission Operation Support Center) system which it expects to finish (at the earliest), December 1999," (*Government Computer News* [April 14, 1997]).

The Russian system operates on the same system our missiles used before GPS, known as gravitational mapping. The Russians and the U.S. both made extensive global maps of these minor fluctuations in the earth's gravitational field. These fluctuations were used to create a map that ICBMs could navigate by. This idea was used for at least 30 years in the United States, and is still in use in Russia. For the first time since shortly after World War II, the United States will no longer be able to respond in the event of a Russian nuclear attack. When GPS goes down in August of 1999, the United States' ICBMs guidance systems will be effectually worthless. The Russians' missile guidance systems, however, will have no such problem. Theirs will be fully functional until at least 2000, when Y2K will create havoc for everyone.

It is this window of opportunity, from August 22 to December 31, 1999, that this author believes the Russians may exploit to finally take the United

States off the world stage. The vast majority of NATO member countries' ICBMs have also been converted to GPS, and will suffer similar failures. The West will literally be without ability to respond in the event of an offensive nuclear attack by the Russians. The balance of power during this window of opportunity will no longer exist. It will tilt completely in Russia's favor. MAD will no longer be in force. They need to take us out of the picture and out of the way if they are to claw their way back to supremacy.

The Implications of a Y2K Meltdown
for the U.S. Military

The damage to the U.S. military of going into the year 2000 with noncompliant systems will be substantial.

Consequences of unrepaired military mainframe, software, PCs, and embedded chips include the following:

- Communications systems may fail
- Satellite positioning errors
- Encryption errors
- Shipboard nuclear shutdowns or malfunctions
- Weapons systems targeting errors
- Torpedo and cruise missile needing guidance repairs
- Military aircraft flight control problems
- Naval vessel recalls to port for upgrades
- Maintenance schedule miscalculations
- Compromised base security
- Command and control system malfunctions

Affected by these problems will be the U.S. Army, Air Force, Navy, Marines, and Coast Guard, as well as the Pentagon and DOD, the CIA, National Security Agency, and other security agencies in America and other western nations that depend largely upon computer-based communications and artificial/electronic intelligence gathering. The Y2K problem will heavily impact our global positioning satellites, weather satellites, radar satellites, communications satellites, the Hubble telescope, and other computer-driven objects floating in space — which will be very difficult to repair. Repairs to military equipment actually deployed and in use are very expensive. It may be necessary to arrange special rotation of submarines, ships, and aircraft to repair facilities to make the necessary year 2000 repairs.

The DOD interacts with the military commands of all other Western nations. If their computers are not compliant, warns Assistant Secretary of Defense Emmette Paige, Jr., then they will send corrupt data into our connected computers. The communications and command systems of America and its European allies may be about to go down. An era of military realignment will follow, and America may well be the loser.

13

Foreign Non-compliance

The Rest of the World Is Far Behind in Y2K Remediation

"If we have everything fixed in the United States, but there's major disruptions in Europe and total calamity in Asia and Latin America, we're going to be affected in a very, very adverse fashion."

— Edward Yardeni

It must be remembered that the Y2K crisis is not just an American problem — it is a global problem. Even if America were miraculously 100 percent compliant by December 31, 1999, the rest of the world is likely to be ill-prepared, which will economically pull down the United States with them. So what is the status of the rest of the world with respect to Y2K compliance?

A recent *Associated Press* survey of businesses, government agencies, and information technology researchers in 16 countries suggests that many nations are only now waking up to the problem. The laggards include Germany, Japan, and Russia — all major players in a closely entwined global economy. A recent World Bank survey found that only 37 of 128 borrowing member nations are even aware of the millennium bug.

The president of the Information Technology Associates of America said recently that the Organization for Economic Cooperation and Development is "acting as if there is no Y2K issue at all." In Goldman Sachs' October 1997 survey of some of Europe's largest companies, none claimed to be fully Y2K compliant; only 43 percent of respondents had completed systems audits; 39 percent could not or did not disclose their expected costs of dealing with Y2K; and 33 percent had not yet secured staff to fix the problem.

As the *Orange County Register* (July 5, 1998) reported, "Even if the United States, the world's most computerized nation, gets the problem fixed, the globalization of economies makes everyone vulnerable to failure outside their borders. Sever a key link — power, finance, telecommunications, medical devices, transportation — even for a few days, and the implications are dire."

The airline industry promises that planes won't fall out of the sky, but radar and air traffic control glitches could make it unsafe to fly over some nations. Telecommunications are also a concern. A survey of 113 countries by the U.S. State Department found that telecommunications companies in 33 countries are having problems with year 2000 fixes and that 29 others are unaware, or have not begun to address, the Y2K problem. At a June 1998 Y2K conference in Thailand, attended by national statistics agencies, representatives from China and Nepal said awareness in their countries is so low that many people think the 2000 bug is just another computer virus.

A recent survey of the Gartner Group found that half of 6,000 companies surveyed in 47 countries will have less than 20 percent of their mission-critical systems fixed and tested in time for 2000. Many of these are smaller companies that are suppliers to larger companies. That's where the cascade effect can occur. Just because a company is prepared doesn't mean its key suppliers or trading partners will be.

Over $3 trillion is transferred electronically on a global basis every day in foreign currency, securities, and derivatives markets. What if 5 percent of those transfers malfunction due to bad computers somewhere in the world? Chaos will quickly reign!

In many European, Asian, and Latin countries, the infrastructure of vital services — electricity, water, telecommunications, postal services, transportation, customs, etc. — and distribution channels may be severely disrupted. Studies of various industries and utilities indicate that urban infrastructures around the world may be weakened considerably at the turn of the century.

In a January 1998 study of potential Y2K impact on Copenhagen, Denmark, Corporation 2000 concluded that the city's power support will likely be disrupted for the first 10 days of the year 2000 and that transportation services will be hampered by fuel and power shortages. The study also predicted that telephone systems will be inoperable in some areas, that hospitals will operate only on an emergency basis, and that schools and banks will be closed for a month. These conclusions were based on assessments of the status of various organizations' Y2K compliance efforts, the failure of which likely would impair the city's commerce, infrastructure, and government.

If Y2K events as disastrous as those identified in that study occur simultaneously in hundreds of cities around the world, a global depression of incredible proportions could be triggered. If power is widely interrupted as long as it recently was in Auckland, New Zealand (four months), the results would be simply catastrophic.

CIA Estimates of Global Y2K Progress

The United States is the country most prepared for the Y2K crisis, with Canada, Australia, and Britain either equal or about six months behind. The rest of western Europe (whose problems are compounded by the introduction of the Euro currency in January 1999) lags nine months behind the United States. After western Europe, according to the CIA's assessment, Japan, China, Hong Kong, and most other Pacific Rim countries are lagging the United States by up to a year in their preparations. CIA officials describe Latin America as being "way behind the power curve."

Foreign Progress on Y2K

Canada

While some could argue that the level of activity in the business sector in Canada lags slightly behind the United States, Canada does lead in two specific areas. The Canadian government, unlike the United States, has taken strong steps, by way of Y2K booklets and print advertising, to communicate the severity of the problem to business in general.

In addition to this lead, the Canadian banking system (with only five major national banks) is structured in such a manner that it was possible to coordinate efforts. Working together in informal meetings, they arrived at solution strategies advantageous to all participants. This collaborative effort has enabled the Canadian banks to be in perhaps the best position worldwide to deal with January 1, 2000. Personal interviews with two of the leading executives of these key banks by Grant Jeffrey confirm the probability that Canada's major banks will be ready.

Great Britain

The well-respected *Intelligence Digest* wrote recently that Great Britain will not be Y2K compliant in time. The latest assessment of computer industry sources is that the United Kingdom can still achieve 65 percent compliance and that this will mean avoiding meltdown "as long as it is the right 65 percent." Currently, only about 16 percent of British public-sector computers are compliant. None of the water and sewage disposal companies are compliant. British Telecom cannot guarantee that it will be compliant. The British government has begun preparing emergency plans along the lines of civil defense plans from the Cold War.

As an example of Y2K problems, one of the British retail giants, Marks & Spencer, destroyed the chain's entire stock of corned beef because all crates and individual cans had been bar-coded with an "02" sell-by date. The computers read that as "1902" and destroyed what it believed was 96-year-old corned beef.

Germany

A June survey of 378 mid-size German companies by Frankfurt-based KHK Software found 57 percent had done nothing to address the year 2000 problem or the impending conversion from the German mark to the European Union's new single currency; only 3 percent had budgeted for it.

France

About 70 percent of France's roughly one million small businesses don't even consider themselves at risk to the Y2K millennium bug, says Jean-Pierre Tanne, information specialist for the Chamber of Commerce and Industry. "They have no methodological approach, no tools, no technical support."

Russia

Only a third of 50 large financial institutions in Russia were aware of the Y2K bug. Many banks erroneously think they will not be affected because their computer hardware is relatively new, says Pat Kellehern, a computer system consultant for Coopers and Lybrand. "There's a worrying trend that seems to suggest the banks don't think they have a problem. I'm not sure they're taking it seriously."

One of Russia's most sensitive industries seems to lack a basic understanding of the dangers. "We don't have any problems yet," the Atomic Energy Ministry's spokesman, Vladislave Petrov, said. "We'll deal with the problem in the year 2000." Russia is a major Y2K concern. In a *Reuters* report on June 29, 1998, the State Telecommunications Committee, assigned to coordinate year 2000 activities in state agencies, stated that repair work began in May 1998. Another report suggests that Russia's Y2K computer repairs will take at least 50 years.

China

China's problems with the 2000 bug are compounded by its reliance on all kinds of software from foreign and Chinese developers and on enormous numbers of Chinese-pirated versions of software. Zhang Qi, the Information Ministry official in charge of her country's efforts to fix the Y2K problem, told the *China Daily* in May that "China hasn't seriously considered the year 2000 glitch."

India

Thousands of Indian programmers are working on year 2000 fixes, but their employers are almost exclusively abroad. However, Indian industry and government haven't fully faced the problem. "We haven't done enough," says Ravindra Gupta, a top official in the Indian Federal Electronics Department.

Australia

The managing director of the Australian Stock Exchange, Richard Humphry, has warned that the Victorian electricity industry may be unable to fix the millennium bug computer problem on time. He says there could be severe power shortages from January 2000 across the national grid.

The National Australia Bank has admitted to the stock exchange that the Y2K problem is far too complex for any business to claim compliance with legitimacy. The Australian government has modeled its activities closely on those implemented in Canada and the United Kingdom. However, given that they started later, they have increased their awareness marketing strategy to include television as well as print media.

Japan

Next to America, Japan is the most highly automated, computer-dependent countries in the world. That they should be ignoring this problem is a cause for concern, perhaps more than the concerns raised by the reports from Russia.

In Japan, the world's second most computerized nation, officials of three major banks — the Bank of Tokyo Mitsubishi, Daichi Kangyo, and Sakura — told the AP that their year 2000 projects are running on schedule. However, the awareness of Y2K and the commitment to solve it are lacking.

A computer expert in Tokyo, Yoshiya Fuhita of NRI Information Systems, said he believes Japanese banks "are in a dangerous state." The country's financial sector lags well behind the United States, spending just one-tenth as much on software fixes, he said. Japan is preoccupied with its current fiscal problems and is seriously falling behind in efforts to head off the Y2K crisis.

Thailand

Thailand has yet to conduct a potential Year 2000 damage assessment, let alone budget funds for repairs. Bangkok officials were horrified to discover in a random Y2K test that all the country's criminal records would have been expunged had they not discovered the problem.

Venezuela

Venezuela's government has not even begun examining its computers to assess what Y2K repairs are needed. "We're in an emergency," warned Edgar Martinez, the country's year 2000 coordinator. Martinez fears a paralysis lasting at least a week, including widespread power outages, a halt for Caracas' subway, and computer failures that could wipe out pension payments, academic records, and payrolls. "We're going to have all kinds of problems," he said.

Foreign Power Grids Also in Danger

As far behind as the U.S. electric power industry seems to be in remediation, foreign power companies and grids are in much worse shape. Joyce Amenta, director of information technology for the United Nations, estimates that over one-third of all nations won't be ready for Y2K.

"Fear will begin to hit next year. People will start to take their money out of the banks," said Amenta on June 30, 1998, "leading to further and further paralysis as we get closer to the date."

Another study released June 30, 1998 by the World Bank said only that 10 percent of 120 nations classified as developing countries have a government-wide Y2K program.

Even if the U.S. and Europe have fixed their computers' Y2K problems, failures in developing countries could affect international currency transfers and securities settlements, according to New York Federal Reserve vice-president Ernest T. Patrikia. In his report to the U.S. House of Representatives Subcommittee on Banking and Finance, Patrikia said, "Nearly all financial organizations worldwide are at risk for Year 2000 problems. Regulators cannot guarantee that Y2K disruptions will not occur — because they will."

14

The Social, Legal, and Global Implications of the Y2K Crisis

The implications of the Y2K crisis for America and our affluent, comfortable way of life are ominous. What will you do if, on New Year's day, 2000, the following happens:

You try to draw money from an ATM at your local bank, and it tells you that you have no account balance, even though you know you have $10,000 in your account. Your bank's computer thinks it's January 1, 1900 and you aren't a customer according to its Y2K-defective records.

The local power plant fails, and it's mid-winter (Northern hemisphere). The power company's production is controlled by some computer chips that were installed many years ago by a company that has now gone out of business. No one knows what they do, how they work, nor do they dare touch them because the whole plant might come to a standstill. This it does obligingly on January 1, 2000.

The air conditioning fails in the southern states.

The telephone system fails — and you're trying to contact someone to find out what's going on.

Your employer has computer-related problems with his suppliers, his banks, his production and administration systems. He lays you off, since he can't get supplies to run his production line (his supplier has computer-related problems) and his bank's computer can't find any record that he has any money in the bank. In addition, his own computer systems have gone haywire, and he can't get money in from customers or check out what his stock levels should be.

The pension agency cannot pay your pension because you have not made any contributions according to their computers. Well, if their computers think it's January 1, 1900, you weren't around then to make any contributions, were you?

The agencies paying unemployment and Social Security cannot make these payments because the records don't show the claimant as being entitled to benefits.

Less money is spent by unemployed people, pensioners, and benefit claimants (they don't have the money to spend). Shops and service companies have to lay off staff, which creates a downward spiral of money being spent in the local community.

The computers in financial services organizations cannot pay dividends to their investors.

There's a drop in the stock markets because of the bad news coming from companies about their inability to trade normally. You sell shares to cut your losses and/or raise needed cash. Will you get paid? Will the selling be self-perpetuating and lead to a 1929-style crash and a subsequent deep recession? Will there be social unrest?

Your medical center's computer has Y2K problems and cannot trace the medicines you've been prescribed in the past, nor the illnesses you've had. Your doctor prescribes the wrong medicine and you become very ill.

The police cannot trace the records of known criminals, nor their fingerprints. Some prisoners are released wrongly.

Airline (and bus and train) schedules go haywire. Airplanes fly without proper maintenance.

Chaos in the Cities

What will happen in major North American cities, where most of the infrastructure is now controlled by computers, if the welfare, Medicare, Medicaid, or other government assistance checks (possibly including Social Security) stop coming; if unemployment skyrockets due to Y2K-induced layoffs; if there are power brownouts or blackouts that take out your lights, heat, city water, traffic lights and communications; if the telephone, fax, email systems fail; and if food deliveries to your city (which only has about 72 hours of food) are halted or dramatically curtailed?

If the crisis lasts more than a few days (i.e., for a few weeks, months, or even a year or more), there likely would be dramatic increases in crime, looting, and urban violence. Hunger, thirst, and disease could spread rapidly. The local governmental officials and law enforcement would quickly lose their control to gangs, martial law would probably be declared (at least in the major cities), much as it was in 1992 during the Los Angeles riots. Under martial law (or a state of emergency), your constitutional rights (including trial by jury) are suspended and the military (federal troops, national guard, UN troops or somebody's troops) keeps order — through the barrel of a gun.

Escape from New York

Edward Yourdon, author of *Time Bomb 2000,* has said that New York could become like Beirut, Lebanon. In his testimony before Congress on November 4, 1997, Ed Yardeni said that in spite of New York City being one of the best prepared (for Y2K) cities in the world, "the city (NYC) still faces massive disruption, for up to a month at the start of the year 2000." This can also be said for hundreds of other lesser-prepared U.S. cities.

According to *Computer Weekly* (September 11, 1997), after reading a report that Y2K will throw New York City into chaos — with power supplies, schools, hospitals, transportation, and the finance sector likely to suffer severe disruptions, the governor of New York state banned all nonessential computer projects so the state can focus on Y2K remediation.

In July 1997, a state official told the New York Year 2000 Use Group that New York was only 5 percent of the way through its millennium projects, projected to cost between $100 million and $185 million. New York City is spending another $300 million to replace its noncompliant budget and accounting system and on fixing or replacing other systems. Despite these efforts, and others made in the private sector, an independent study of New York's infrastructure has estimated that the city still faces massive disruption for up to a month at the start of the year 2000.

The study, carried out by the UK-based Corporation 2000, expects the city's hospitals to be reduced to accepting emergency cases only, and schools to be closed for up to a month. Power supplies and telecommunications are only expected to be available at half the normal levels and banks and the stock market will be shut down for up to eight days, according to the study.

The Legal Implications of the Y2K Crisis

We live today in a litigious country, where everyone sues anyone for anything as a form of legal plunder. We are all familiar with the multibillion-dollar legal settlements in recent years regarding asbestos, silicon implants, and tobacco, not to mention the ridiculous settlements — like McDonald's Restaurants being ordered to pay $3 million to a customer who spilled a cup of hot coffee on herself. But these settlements are nothing, compared to the wave of Y2K litigation that is coming. Legal costs of over $1 trillion are now being forecast for the U.S. alone.

The *Kansas City Business Journal* (October 27, 1997) carried an interesting article by lawyer Matt Swafford entitled "Millennium Bug Raises Potential for Legal Consequences":

> In the first week of May 1997, the 10 cash registers owned by a Detroit-area produce supplier crashed more than 100 times, crippling the business. The reason? The software used to run the registers could not handle sales billed to credit cards expiring in the year 2000.
>
> The result? The produce supplier sued the cash

register maker in the first United States litigation arising from the so-called Millennium Bug.

It will not be the last. Jeff Jinnett, an expert on Millennium Bug claims, recently told a group of Lloyd's of London underwriters that the claims arising from the Bug will likely exceed $1 trillion dollars in the U.S. alone. Compare this to the roughly $300 billion forecast for all liabilities unrelated to the Bug, including asbestos, pollution and general torts, and one begins to get a sense of the potential scope of the problem.

"Aside from the Bug's enormous potential for business disruption, the possible legal liabilities are also quite real."

Contracts: If something your business produces fails because of the Y2K Bug, the business is potentially liable under both express and implied warranties, unless the warranties are adequately disclaimed. Other businesses may be affected as well. For example, a manufacturer whose assembly line or shipping department is shut down by the Bug could face liability for breach of contract in failing to meet contract deadlines.

Financial Disclosures: Nearly all businesses must make some form of financial disclosures, be they in annual reports, credit applications or elsewhere. The failure to disclose the reasonably anticipated costs to your business of both fixing the Bug and dealing with the non-fixable problems caused by the Bug could result in a distorted financial snapshot. Failure to make these disclosures could subject companies to fines or tort liability, and could lead to investor suits.

Copyrights: The unauthorized modification of a piece of copyrighted software to avoid the Millennium Bug could constitute the preparation of a derivative work, subjecting the business to a claim of copyright infringement or breach of the license agreement.

Other Liabilities: Parties to a transaction who fail to disclose or account for problems arising from the Millennium Bug could face liability under many theories, including breach of contract, professional malpractice and negligence. The failure of the officers or directors of a company to make and implement a plan could lead to claims by investors.

The millennium is almost upon us, and, while the Y2K problem most likely will not cause a complete technological apocalypse, it will have a significant and lasting impact on commerce. It is the nature of our society that people who lose money due to the effects of the Bug will look for others to blame. The resulting litigation has already begun, a year before the millennium itself. With proper planning now, however, it is still possible to minimize the bug's potential effects on your business.

Eleven Thought-provoking Questions to Answer Before 1999

Dr. Gary North is one of the country's most prolific writers warning about the Y2K problem. He recently asked his readers to answer the following questions before 1999. They are interesting food for thought.

1) What happens to the world's financial markets if 1 percent of the transactions have incorrect figures? For example, the international currency markets trade over $1 trillion in currencies every day. A 1 percent error rate means that $10 billion in daily entries will be wrong. Every day, day after day. These losses will become cumulative.

2) If depositors in 1999 hear rumors that the big banks' computers will not be fixed in time, will they keep all of their money in the local bank, risking it all for 4 percent per year, or will they begin withdrawing cash? If they withdraw most of their cash and refuse to redeposit it, the world's banking system will collapse — the effect of fractional reserve banking. The central banks will have to print piles of paper money; mass inflation in the cash markets with complete collapse of prices (deflation) in the credit markets (stocks, bonds) will result.

3) If sellers of goods and services begin to demand cash from buyers, will you and your neighbors withdraw cash from your bank accounts?

4) If the banks close, how will governments collect taxes?

5) If governments cannot collect taxes, what will happen to the value of government bonds, T-bills, and other forms of government debt?

6) If U.S. T-bills fall in value, what will happen to the liquidity and value of all those "secure money market funds" that are heavily invested in T-bills?

7) If U.S. Treasury paper falls in value, will foreign central banks continue to hold Treasury paper instead of

gold, or will there be a gold rush by central banks and other informed investors?

8) If foreign investors start selling dollar-denominated U.S. debt, what will happen to interest rates in the United States? When interest rates rise sharply, businesses go bankrupt rapidly. It's called a depression. It will be world-wide.

9) If the nation's railroads don't get their own computers year-2000 compliant and 100 percent integrated with all of the other railroads' computers, what happens to the delivery of coal, grain, and industrial chemicals? A 1 percent failure rate per month — lost freight cars, train accidents — will have negative effects on sellers' willingness to put their goods on trains. Think very carefully about your city's vulnerability.

10) If predictable food delivery by the railroads is called into question, what will happen to today's full shelves in your local supermarket? The average food market has to be restocked every 72 hours.

11) If truckers don't think they will be paid in cash, why will they take the risk of making deliveries into cities? If there is urban rioting, the answer is obvious.

The Y2K Crisis: An Opportunity for Global Socialists?

A few years ago, David Rockefeller, one of the major globalist leaders, said, "We are on the verge of a global transformation. All we need is the right major crisis and the nations will accept the New World Order."

The socialists of our day use crises and crisis management to impose on citizens socialist solutions and laws that would never be tolerated without the crisis. Some of these crises are manufactured (money laundering; child abuse; guns; the environment; global warming, etc.), and some are real. The millennium bug crisis is real. It may be the biggest crisis to hit western civilization in centuries — with the exceptions of World War I and II. And the globalists will use it to advance their agenda if they can.

Already, many world leaders are talking about the only way to save the world from this global threat is a united global effort with a "global czar" to be placed in charge of one united, coordinated effort to save the planet. A government Y2K conference was recently held in Washington to address the Y2K problem. The title of the conference was, "Drastic Measures for Drastic Times: Government Agency Assessment, Testing, Conversion, and Best Practices for Year 2000 Compliance."

The keynote speech was given by Robert Bemes, who is known as the father of the ASCII code for computers. He created the concept of timesharing (which made the Internet possible), the concept of word processing, and he coined the term "COBOL." In addition, he created the first load-and-go compiler and one of the first date-compression methods for communications.

He discussed in detail the serious problems with the "quick fixes" that have been proposed to temporarily fix the Y2K problem. Perhaps most intriguing, however, is the solution he proposed to fix the problem worldwide:

> We must have national direction! I can say this with total sincerity, while still believing in minimal government . . . So is there another Churchill in view? Someone has to be in direct and sole charge, without any other assignments to worry about. The name I have heard is Mikhail Gorbachev. Sounds

good to me. He doesn't owe us much, and can't be bribed . . .

If we can have a summit on global warming (which seems suspect, anyway), we should certainly have a global summit on the Year 2000 problem. If such could be mounted, it would ease the way to get someone of Mr. Gorbachev's standing to be czar. What is the United Nation's position on this? Have they even discussed it? If not, why not take this world problem there for action?

Curiously, when the House Information and Technology Subcommittee (chaired by Congressman Stephen Horn) held hearings on the Y2K issue in Los Angeles on October 17, 1997, the only witness to testify was Mikhail Gorbachev. The former Communist dictator of the Soviet Union has become the leader of the Y2K awareness/repair program in Russia. Could this be a stepping stone towards becoming Y2K czar for the world? This is believed to be the first time that a Russian or Soviet president has ever testified to Congress, according to a congressional spokesman.

Since people-control is high on the agenda of the global socialists, and computers are a major tool that the socialists hope to use to number, watch, track, and control people, a breakdown in the world computer systems would seem to be a major setback for the people-controllers. However, if a Rockefeller, a Kissinger, a Gorbachev, or a Bill Gates-type from the globalist establishment could emerge with a solution to this global crisis (or falsely "claim" to have such a solution), great riches and political power would accrue to that person or group.

Barring a simple "silver-bullet" solution to Y2K, which does not seem to be on the horizon, the global socialists can still be expected to try and use the Y2K crisis, and the global disruptions it is likely to cause, as an excuse to grab even more power and move us toward a world government.

15

The Clinton Administration's Response to Y2K

The U.S. government is unique amongst the leaders in this [Y2K] race in that they have made no organized attempt to communicate the nature of the problem to the masses. Their activities compare poorly to the Canadians, U.K., Australian, South African, and Dutch governments, who have all made varying attempts to communicate to businesses and the public the severity of the problem and the necessity for immediate action.

U.S. government activities have concerned themselves with internal matters only and have left business to its own devices. Needless to say, because of this inaction, the presidential race in the Year 2000 should be interesting, given that the computer problem cannot help but become a volatile election issue.

— *Wall Street Journal* (July 14, 1998)

I firmly believe that everything has a reason and purpose behind it, that very few things are simply accidental, and that there are definite, well-calculated reasons behind President Clinton's and Vice President Gore's near silence and inaction on Y2K.

The Clinton/Gore silence and inactivity on Y2K is strange. A growing number of members of Congress and even the media have begun to criticize Gore and Clinton for their passive approach to Y2K. British prime minister Tony Blair's activism on Y2K stands out in stark contrast to the Clinton/Gore silence. As Howard Rubin, a professor at the City University of New York and a leading government consultant on the Y2K program, expressed it to Arnaud de Borchgrave in a recent interview with the *Washington Times*: "The government doesn't have a clue. I have told Vice President Gore that the 2000 election will turn on whatever disasters the Year 2000 crisis brings. To appear passive now is a recipe for defeat."

Frank Gaffney, head of the Center for Security Policy, also observed the Clinton/Gore inactivity and passivity on Y2K:

The "buck" for this deplorable state of affairs clearly stops with the Clinton Administration — and most especially, its nominal point man on technical issues in general, and computer issues in particular, Vice President Al Gore.

If for no other reason but simple self-interest, it behooves Vice President Gore to devote some of the personal energy and political capital he is currently devoting to global warming — a problem that is, in all likelihood, no problem at all — and apply them towards meeting an impending and genuine catastrophe. It will be a measure of the man and his fitness for the highest office in the land if he continues to be AWOL on the Millennium Bug. More to the point, as Dr. Rubin observes, he may not even be a viable candidate for the Presidency if, 11 months before the election, his palpable failure of leadership becomes a nightmare for virtually every American.

Reasons for the Clinton/Gore Silence and Passivity about the Y2K Crisis

There are several possible reasons for the administration's inactivity on Y2K:

1) Wall Street and the Establishment may be counseling Clinton to be low key on Y2K for the moment to give them a chance to bail out of the market.

The big guys — the top management in the Merrill Lynchs, the Dean Witters, the Goldman Sachs, etc. — are rumored to be bailing out. They see the "rogue wave" coming, but they need time (another three or four months) to get out of the markets. So do many of the top management, the CEOs, the board members, the insiders in the huge multinational corporations who have been steadily selling their stocks over the past year.

The middle class, the little guy, must keep plunging into the market with his or her life savings and retirement funds in order to give the big guys (who definitely see the trouble ahead) someone to sell their stock to. So the financial news must be kept positive, Y2K must be downplayed, and the public must be kept in their "be happy/don't worry" frame of mind for at least a few more months — even if it means a bigger than ever panic later. The media has cooperated well in this downplaying of Y2K — at least until very recently. So has Alan Greenspan and the Fed with very limited, muted statements regarding Y2K.

2) Clinton/Gore and their Establishment comrades may be intentionally setting the stage for a panic and the declaration of a state of national emergency and martial law sometime in 1999.

It should never be forgotten that Clinton, Gore, Hillary, and the top echelon of the administration are dedicated leftists (socialists) who aspire to great power (getting it and keeping it) and control over the people. They are also globalists who dream of a world government in which they are major players.

Could it be that they do not want the Y2K crisis to be solved in America? Could it be that Y2K could be that "right major crisis" that David Rockefeller talked about a few years ago, wherein the people would happily yield their freedom and sovereignty to a world government? Could it be that Clinton/Gore are planning a State of National Emergency and martial law to deal with the crisis sometime in 1999?

Is it possible that they will use this "emergency" to further their agenda, to attack and silence the right wing as they did after the Oklahoma City bombing, push gun control, and other people-control measures that would never get through Congress or be accepted by the people in normal times? Could it be that they have no intention for national elections to be held in 2000 because Bill, Al, and Hillary see themselves as "more permanent-type leaders" for America in the new millennium?

3) Is the recent avalanche of Clinton executive orders tied to a Y2K-related state of emergency?

Since Bill Clinton came to office in 1993, there have been dozens of new executive orders signed by the president, especially during the past year. These are, of course, unconstitutional acts that allow the President to circumvent the will and constraints of the Congress. Hitler used such orders throughout the 1930s to amass great power. Over the past year or so, Clinton has moved FEMA (Federal Emergency Management Agency) out from under the authority of the Congress and under the National Security Council (under Clinton's authority). FEMA is the agency that would be responsible for implementing a state of emergency.

On June 6, 1994, President Clinton signed Executive Order #12919, which gathers together into a single document the authority of 11 preceding executive orders (from 1939 through 1991) issued by former presidents. Those orders, if invoked, would virtually suspend the Constitution. This consolidation of executive authority invests FEMA (Federal Emergency Management Agency) with absolute power over the following:

• All U.S. communications facilities (EO 10995)
• Electrical power, petroleum, gas, fuels and minerals, private and public (EO 10997)
• Food supplies, agricultural lands and facilities (EO 10998)
• Transportation of any kind, including private vehicles,

and control of seaports, waterways, and highways (EO 10999)

• Civilian labor forces, without regard to financial remuneration as authorized under the "Defense Production Act of 1930" (EO 11000)

• Health, education, and welfare institutions (EO 11001)

• All airport and air transportation, public, private, and commercial (EO 11003)

• Housing and Finance Authority for purposes of relocating communities, building new housing with public funds, designating areas to be abandoned, and establishing new locations for populations.

• Railroads, inland waterways, and public storage facilities (EO 11003)

• A national registration compiled by the postmaster general, of all residents of the U.S. for purposes of controlling population movement and relocation (EO 11002)

• Enforcement of the plans set out in these executive orders by the Department of Justice (EP 11310)

All of the Executive Orders (EO) from January 1961 through the present, may be reviewed on the Internet at www.legal.gsa.gov/legal1geo.html. This site will give you the number (all are in numerical order), title, date signed, and who (i.e. White House, GSA, etc.) signed them. You can also retrieve the entire text of the Executive Orders. It's amazing how many were signed by the "White House" since January 20, 1993.

All of the powers mentioned above can be invoked with the stroke of the president's pen, and are free of congressional restrictions or intervention for a period of six months. President Clinton boasted early in his presidency (and in recent months) that if Congress did not cooperate with him, he would simply run the country by executive orders. He has lived up to his word, issuing more executive orders than any president in the history of this nation — and he's not finished yet.

Chuck Missler recently wrote in his *Intelligence Briefing* about Clinton's newest executive order, #13011, signed on July 16, 1998, which creates a gargantuan new bureaucracy with authority to manage "Federal Information Technology":

It links the data gathered by the Health, Education, and Labor Departments (the data bases created through the school systems) to the data accessible to the FBI, CIA, EPA, and other federal agencies. And it apparently gives this unified information system unspecified power to propagandize the public by disseminating politically correct information everywhere; to control people through a vast federal data bank and monitoring system.

The "major government mission areas" of this executive order include electronic commerce, law enforcement, environmental protection, national defense, and health care. In the name of national security and protection from terrorists, polluters, extremists, and other enemies to the global village, the all-seeing eyes of the State will have power to search everywhere and to monitor everyone.

Section 7 links the federal information management system to "state and local governments" and "nongovernmental international organizations" and "intergovernmental organizations."

Section 9 deals with "liaison, consultation, and

negotiation with foreign governments and inter-governmental organizations on all matters related to information resources management" and ensures "that the United States is represented in the development of international standards . . . affecting information technology."

Standing alone, this executive order might raise little alarm. But examined in the light of the United Nations agenda and stated government intentions, it looks ominous. The UN has called for a sophisticated international computerized information system that would disseminate its politically correct data and pseudo-scientific risk assessments into every community, build consensus based on its visions, goals, values, and choices, then monitor individual and collective compliance everywhere — in homes, schools, offices . . .

"Develop gender-sensitive databases, information and monitoring systems," states the Beijing Platform for Action (#258). It calls for the "consistent flow of information" among "national, subre-gional/regional and international institutions." (#288) — all under the watchful guidance of the UN Social and Economic Council.

There are other executive orders signed by Clinton over the past year, which, taken together with all of his executive orders signed since 1993, set up the potential machinery for a coming state of national emergency or a virtual dictatorship.

Most other nations, including the United Kingdom and Canada, have enacted similar emergency laws as

Orders in Council that allow the government to rule by decree in a declared "national emergency."

16

Conclusion and Recommendations: Don't Worry! Be Prepared!

The computer professionals in the trenches, who are trying to fix the millennium bug, all agree on the following: At the present rate of progress, there will be interruptions of public and private services (how many and for how long they don't know, but they fear the worst). There will be many business failures, particularly among small- to medium-sized companies. Much of the federal government (including some of its largest agencies) will not be Y2K compliant, causing major problems in 2000 and beyond.

Foreign governments, businesses, and banks are in far worse shape regarding remediation of Y2K than in America and Canada — particularly in Japan and the rest of Asia. Europe is preparing, but is far behind because of its preoccupation with the change to a new currency (the

Euro) in 1999 — a massive computerized, bureaucratic, and financial undertaking.

The Y2K experts believe that the telephone and transportation systems, water and sewage treatment facilities, chemical plants, oil refineries, nuclear power plants, and U.S. military weapons systems are also at risk. They believe that, in the sobering words of one IBM executive who is working on fixing some of the 400,000 AS/400 computers, "The international banking system is about to go into the toilet."

Compounding the problem is the fact that the space-saving two-digit-year is also embedded in the embedded microchips and software that run most of the world's manufacturing plants. Global positioning equipment, telephone systems, nuclear energy plants, bank vaults, heating and cooling systems, military weapons systems, water and sewer systems, oil refineries, and even desktop and laptop computers are equally vulnerable.

Experts disagree as to how many of the 40 billion chips now in use worldwide may have the embedded two-digit-year date. The optimists say 5 percent; the pessimists say 25 percent. These chips are embedded in equipment all over the world, and no one knows which ones are Y2K compliant and which ones are not. Finding the bad ones is like finding (or avoiding) the bullet in a deadly game of Russian roulette — a lot of luck is involved.

What happens if many of the computers (or chips) in the world malfunction, crash, or start spitting out garbled data? The whole world financial system and economy would go into instant gridlock and then crash. But what if just a few percent of them failed? What would be the impact of just a 1 percent failure across America and all around the world? A strike at just one brake manufacturing plant brought North American automobile production at 29 General Motors plants to a sudden halt. One computerized software glitch shut down AT&T's entire Northeastern network.

The Y2K pessimists are not saying that the Y2K problem cannot be solved. They are saying that every system cannot be fixed in time because the problem is too big and the world (due to ignorance, apathy, complacency, procrastination, or denial) has delayed the work on the problem until it is far too late to solve it by the December 31, 1999 deadline.

What should you do with this information about the Y2K crisis?

1) One can ignore it in the hope that it will go away or that its potential to disrupt life is greatly exaggerated.

2) One can make moderate preparations in one's business and personal affairs: try to solve or mitigate one's own computer problems; become more conservatively positioned financially; and make some preparations for temporary inconveniences wrought by systems failures (power, light, heating, telecommunications, etc.).

3) One can make massive changes in one's lifestyle and major preparations for self-sufficiency that would be beneficial if the Y2K crisis causes a long-term economic, financial, social, or even political breakdown in America.

Most Americans will simply ignore the problem and do nothing. Some will take moderate precautions, and even fewer will make dramatic changes in their lifestyles. As Proverbs 27:12 says, "The prudent see danger and take refuge, but the simple" will "keep going and suffer for it."

Preparing for the Millennium Y2K Crisis:
Getting Out of Harm's Way

The first step in preparing oneself and family for the Y2K crisis is to fully understand the problem. The better you understand it, the more motivated you will be to take serious protective measures. At first you may have a sense of being overwhelmed at how much you have to do, how much it will cost, and how long it will take. But as the Chinese proverb says, "the journey of a thousand miles starts with the first step. . . ." Sit down with your family, discuss the challenge, and make a list of what is important. Pray about your priorities and then develop a family plan for implementing that prioritized list. Some guidelines that may help you in your planning process follow:

Evaluate Your Location

If you're in the city, should you stay? What are the alternatives? Move 50–75 miles from the city and commute to work? Move to the country or a small town and find new work or start a new business? Stay put and hunker down? Get a retreat property several hours or more from the city? Location is your first major decision — everything else flows from this decision.

If the millennium Y2K crisis is as bad as the pessimists believe it could be, major U.S. cities (with populations over 100,000) will be plagued with riots, crime, gang warfare, food shortages, and, if the power grid should fail, no electricity or water. I have long advocated moving to the country or a small town for many reasons, but the potential upheaval from the Y2K problems now makes such a move more important than ever. Major cities could go into gridlock and become very dangerous after the year 2000 arrives.

A rural setting, a few hundred miles from a large city, that provides a well and the ability to grow food or obtain food from local farmers or ranchers will be very important. Alternate heating and energy sources (a wood stove and a backup generator) are vital.

An Escape Plan

For those who are forced to live in an urban area because of their job or other constraints, this might be the time to put together a plan for temporarily relocating to a small town, cottage, or other shelter. It might even pay to sell a city home, rent another, and put the equity into a much less expensive property in a small town. While real estate is overpriced in most cities and suburbs, homes in a number of rural areas can be purchased for surprisingly low prices.

Protect Your Financial Assets

Consider the following suggestions: get out of debt; get liquid; budget and save; monitor the condition of your bank, S&L, and insurance company; get out of all stocks, long bonds (including all municipal bonds), and equity mutual funds; reduce real estate holdings to 25 percent of your net worth and pay off mortgage debt if possible; acquire precious metals, up to a third of your investment portfolio; utilize very short-term T-bills or T-bill money market funds for a large portion of liquid assets; develop a second source of income (a home-based cottage business); utilize Swiss annuities, etc. For more information or assistance in implementing these strategies, call International Collectors Associates at 1-800-525-9556.

If the power grid goes down, the ATMs will not work. You may wish to have three to six months' supply of cash on hand. Develop a strategy that fits the times, maintain a sense of urgency, and pursue that strategy with a sense of urgency — now!

Cash

Federal Reserve notes will be in big demand during a Y2K shutdown. The banking system has a long way to go before their mainframes and software are totally Y2K-compliant. Federal Reserve chairman Alan Greenspan admitted that his agency is prepared to bail out banks in the event of major problems in 2000.

Under today's fractional reserve system, banks lend out anywhere from 95 to 98 percent of all deposits. Of the little that remains, only a portion of it is kept as cash in the vaults. In the event of a Y2K financial panic, there would be almost no cash available. Depositors would line up at banks as they did in the Depression, hoping to withdraw even a small percentage of their deposits (unless the provisions of the Banking Act are implemented and their cash is locked up in the banks).

In order to prevent a nationwide bank run, the government could declare a bank holiday, as Franklin D. Roosevelt did in March 1933, or freeze all accounts via presidential executive order. If that were to happen, paper money would be a highly sought-after commodity for at least a short time. Even though Federal Reserve notes are fiat currency (not backed by gold or silver), they are almost universally considered to be "cash" by the general populace. In a crisis, people will seek something familiar and what they believe to be most valuable. For now, that means U.S. dollars.

Over the longer term, after the initial Y2K crisis, the government may invalidate all circulating cash to punish "speculators" or "currency hoarders" who profited by their foresight. Such a possibility suggests you might be wise to own another asset that can be personally and privately held. Gold and silver coins are the obvious choices for maintaining purchasing power in a small, compact, portable, hideable, highly liquid form. Call International Collectors Associates at 1-800-525-9556 for more information.

Acquire Food Reserves With Extended Shelf Life

Your supplies should include the following: freeze-dried/dehydrated food; bulk grains (corn, white rice, wheat, pinto and navy beans, oats, salt, sugar, and honey); a large garden or greenhouse, if possible, with a large supply of nonhybrid (reproducible) seeds (available from Pinetree Garden Seeds, Box 300, New Gloucester, ME 04260 and R H Schumway, Box 1, Granitville, SC 29829); gardening tools; and, if you live in or near the country, equipment to fish and hunt.

Get to know farmers or ranchers who will sell or barter their produce to you. Keep your food storage program private — known only to your immediate family or closest friends.

In addition to a garden or greenhouse, every family should have at least one year's supply of dehydrated or freeze-dried food reserves. (Two years would be better.) If the U.S. financial system collapses, if you lose your job, if your company closes down, or if food deliveries to cities should be halted or restricted, food reserves will be essential — even life-saving. For more information and free literature about acquiring food reserve systems, call International Collectors Associates at 1-800-525-9556.

Acquire Adequate Clothing

Acquire adequate clothing, particularly for cold weather, when the heat may be off. Long underwear (Capolene is excellent), sweaters, coats, gloves, wool hats, high quality foot gear, leather work gloves, work boots, and protective clothing (coveralls, overalls, etc.). Store several wool army blankets for each member of the family and a dozen more for unprepared friends or relatives who show up on your doorstep at the eleventh hour.

Acquire Alternate Heat, Energy, and Light Sources

If your household appliances are all electric, consider converting all or part of your appliances like dryers, water heater, and stove to either liquid propane or natural gas. That will mean installing a gas tank on your property. Buy or lease the largest tank possible and keep it topped-off monthly. Consider an LP-operated freezer or refrigerator. Buy an electric generator, preferably one with multi-fuel capacity like a combination LP and diesel generator. Buy one between 8–12 Kwh, if possible.

Electric generators are not practical for everyone. Buy alternative heating devices like kerosene heaters, and store extra fuel for it. An outdoor gas grill with a burner to boil water might be a less costly and more practical way to cook. Don't use camp stoves designed for outdoor use indoors. Plan for numerous power outages in the initial months of the year 2000. Knowledgeable government insiders believe they could last up to 90 days. Purchase oil or kerosene lamps with plenty of spare parts, extra wicks, and additional oil or kerosene. Aladdin lamps are excellent.

Buy extra flashlights, extra bulbs, and lots of alkaline batteries of all sizes for radios, clocks and other battery-operated products. Hand-pumped flashlights that don't require batteries are useful. Obtain a large supply of 50-hour long-burning candles, matches, and cigarette lighters for reliable fire starters. Buy some light sticks that safely provide illumination for up to 12 hours.

Additional Fuel Storage

Check with a local agricultural supply house or local farmers and ranchers. Many have used fuel tanks that are no longer in use that they may be glad to get rid of if you will haul them. Diesel fuel is more stable than gasoline, stores better and longer, plus it is less explosive. Be sure you place any fuel storage tanks in a safe area, far away from your home and any machinery that might spark or ignite your fuel. Gasoline or diesel tanks that hold 300 or 500 gallons (the kind you see standing on stilts in farmers' and ranchers' yards in the country) can be bought from agricultural supply stores in small towns and should be refilled monthly.

Obtain a wood stove or wood stove fireplace insert for heat, and acquire several cords of hardwood as soon as possible. A good wood stove can heat 2,000 sq. ft. of living space. LOPI stoves burn both wood and pellets. You can also buy stove fans that move the heated air to increase the heat provided.

Consider solar power. A good source of solar equipment (You 2 Can Be Electrically Independent Solar

Survival Kits for power blackouts, brownouts, and short-ages) is Kent Morgan, 8534 E. 37th Place, Suite 200, India-napolis, IN 46226 (317-465-8496; email at smorgan@saver.com).

Develop Alternate Water Storage, Purification, and Sanitation Sources

Acquire adequate water storage and water purification tablets and filters for every member of your family. Over-capacity here may be a positive move, since you can live for weeks without food, but you will die very quickly without water. It takes a minimum of ½ to 1 gallon of water per day to survive, not including water for bathing, cooking, or for cleaning. If you live in the country, or have a well, you will need backup pumps, parts, and some alternative form of power to get the water out of the ground. You should try to plan for two gallons of stored water daily for each member of your family for several weeks at least.

Fifty-five-gallon water storage containers (drums), with a pumping device are a good way to store a limited amount of water for a short-term emergency, although they are bulky and difficult to move when full of water. Be sure to have plenty of five-gallon portable water jugs. Military water containers are the best, but Wal-Mart and other stores carry commercial containers for campers. Five-gallon containers can be used for ease of handling. If your well goes out, or is contaminated, you will need back-up storage and some means to purify it with either water purification tablets or water filters.

Water purification is the key to long-term survival. You simply can't store enough water in most cases, but if you have water purification equipment, you will have an ongoing supply of water under any situation. Water filters today can literally purify swamp and sewer water. They should be obtained now while they are still available. Katadyn, Pur, and Sweetwater are a few of the best brand names. Purchase a portable filter unit for each member of your family, and get one or two counter-top drip models if possible. This is the only way you will have adequate water to bathe, drink, and cook. If you store water, an excellent way to preserve it and keep it potable is to add one tablespoon of 3 percent hydrogen peroxide per gallon, keep it tightly closed, and in a cool place. It will store indefinitely.

If you live in an area where it is difficult to store water, or you do not have a well, consider a large water tank that you can place on a trailer or in the bed of a truck so you have a mobile supply. Military "water buffalo" trailers are a good solution for some. They hold 400 gallons or more, some are insulated, and they are designed to handle the load. Such a trailer can be used to shuttle water from the source to your home, retreat, etc. As long as you have the means to purify and pump water without electricity, you will be in good shape.

Don't forget to provide for disposal and sanitation of human waste and gray water. Americans take for granted that the toilet will flush every time you use it. If the power grid goes down, municipal sewage may back up or be shut down before it becomes a health hazard. Have some extra water on hand to flush toilets, portable toilets with chemicals to neutralize waste, or some other backup plan. The misery level rises rapidly when forced to endure intolerable stench. Personal hygiene is critically important in any survival situation, no matter the duration. Don't ignore basic sanitation. Purchase ample supplies of toilet paper, soap, etc., in advance.

Develop an Alternative Communications System

Acquire a shortwave/world-band radio receiver to stay up with world and national news in a crisis (and also to tune in to talk radio). Sony has an excellent model that is about the size of a deck of cards. Grundig is another excellent brand. Obtain small hand-held two-way short-wave radios (transceivers) for each member of your family who is 15 years old and up. These small hand-held radios will transmit 10 to 15 miles. A general class amateur license or technician-class amateur license is required. In time of national crisis, these radios may be very useful. Small hand-held walkie-talkies can communicate on citizen band about a half mile. Transceivers on amateur radio frequencies can communicate up to 10 miles. A scanner can help you keep abreast of local developments. Several excellent sources of this kind of equipment are: 1) Ham Radio Outlet (800-854-6046); 2) Amateur Electronic Supply (800-558-0411); 3) Texas Towers (800-272-3467); 4) Radio Shack sells transceivers for citizens band. Radios that run on solar or hand-crank power can also be purchased.

Make Emergency Medical Preparations

Put together or acquire a good emergency first-aid kit with bandages, antibiotics, pain killers, gauze, safety pins, ace bandages, Band-aids, anti-bacterial ointment, and a large quantity of herbal remedies, preferably in tincture form, which retain their potency the longest. Store up cayenne pepper (powder or tincture), which has a host of applications including stopping bleeding and arresting a heart attack. Slippery elm powder is excellent for stomach problems, for dysentery, and as a food supplement.

American Botanical Pharmacy is an excellent source of very pure, very high strength herbs (P.O. Box 3027, Santa Monica, CA 90408 [310-453-1987]). Also keep white willow bark, ginger, Barley Green, rice bran, and Hawthorne berry syrup on hand. Store up extra medicines you are using now and extra vitamins. Buy an extra pair of eyeglasses if you use them. Extra supplies of critical medicines like insulin should be on hand also. Natural health substances with the longest shelf life of all plants are essential oils.

These herbal anti-microbial, anti-viral, anti-bacterial, anti-fungal properties are so powerful they can nourish, strengthen, repair, and sustain life like no other substance known to man. They should be part of your Y2K medical preparations. For a personalized family health kit, call The Essential Oils Healthline at 602-430-7700, or Essential Oils Health Care at 602-430-3300.

Acquire an Emergency Preparedness Library

Stock your library with how-to books on everything from A to Z, including basic first aid, water purification techniques, wild game butchering, auto repair, disposal of waste, the basics of electricity, alternate communications methods, on hiding valuables, and food preservation.

Acquire Hand Tools for Gardening, Carpentry, Car Repair

Buy good-quality tools even if you have to pay more for them. Write or call for Lehman's Non-Electric Catalogue ($3.00), P.O. Box 321, Kidron, Ohio 44636 (1-330-857-5757).

Acquire Alternate Transportation

In the event that the transportation system goes down for a long time and fuel becomes scarce or unavailable, consider bicycles, mountain bikes, motor scooters, trail bikes, ATV quadrunners, or motorcycles. Some of these vehicles use fuel, but in very small amounts.

Stock a Supply of Extra Dry Goods

The following items should be in your inventory: toilet paper, feminine hygiene products, toothpaste, tooth brushes, dental floss, household cleaners, soap, shampoo, paper towels, solvents, razors, shaving cream, lots of large heavy plastic garbage bags, baking soda for odors and cooking, paper, pencils or pens, light bulbs.

Miscellaneous Products that Might Prove Useful

Agricultural lime for sanitation purposes; a wash tub and a wringer; lots of duct tape; laundry disks if soap is scarce (the discs can do hundreds of loads with little or no soap); if you garden, you will need canning jars and related supplies; a hand grinder for corn, wheat, and other grains; cast-iron cookware that can be used on stoves or open fires; fire extinguishers; a sewing kit with polyester thread; 3 percent hydrogen peroxide for water purification; several heavy wool blankets for each member of your family or good, warm sleeping bags that can withstand temperatures down to zero.

Barter Items You Might Wish to Acquire

There are five criteria that qualify an item for barter: 1) high consumer demand; 2) something that is not easily home-manufactured; 3) durable in storage; 4) divisible in small quantities; and 5) authenticity that is easily recognizable. A list of possible barter items follows (no one will acquire all or even most of them, but a few might make sense): liquid detergent; laundry detergent; rubbing alcohol; bleach; toothbrushes; razor blades; toilet paper; aluminum foil; writing paper, typing paper, pens, pencils, erasers; shoelaces, string, cord, rope; fishing line; insect repellent; water repellent; paint, varnish; matches; watches; tape; light bulbs; needles, thread, zippers, buttons; aspirin, vitamins, other drugs; seeds, grain, sugar; coffee, liquor, cigarettes; antibiotics, burn ointments; safety pins; manual can opener; knives; canning jars, lids, rings; shoes, boots, socks, nylon stockings; underwear; winter clothes; coats; blankets; fuels (all types); quarts of multi-vis motor oil; anti-freeze; wire; glues; bolts, screws, nails.

Recommended Books and Resources

America's Last Call: On the Brink of Financial Holocaust by David Wilkerson, Pastor of Times Square Church, New York (P.O. Box 260, Lindale, Texas 75771).

Biblical Guide to Health and Happiness - a monthly newsletter by Salem Kirban giving a Biblical approach to alternate medicine and health for unstable times (Second Coming Missions, 650 Willow Valley Square/K-107, Lancaster, PA 17602-4872).

Two Books on Privacy and Legal Rights: 1) *Bulletproof Privacy: How to Live Happily, Hidden, and Free* ($20.00) and 2) *You and the Police: A Guide to Your Legal Rights* ($16.00) by B. T. Party. Buy the two books for $30.00. Call 1-800-380-2230.

Financial Preparation

1) Get out of debt —totally, if at all possible.

2) Get out of big city real estate — Urban real estate prices will implode in the coming upheaval, and you may be unable to sell at any price. Consider what happened to Los Angeles real estate prices (down 50 percent in some areas of Southern California) after the huge Los Angeles riots of 1992.

3) Get out of the U.S. stock market and equity mutual funds — As soon as possible, get your IRAs, Keoghs, SEPs and other retirement funds out of stocks and long bonds and place these assets either in very short-term Treasury bills, a T-Bill money market fund (six-month maturities or less), or gold coins.

4) Monitor the financial condition of your bank, S&L, and insurance company with a Weiss research report — If your institution is rated C– or lower, switch to a stronger one. To obtain a current rating, call 1-800-525-9556.

5) Accumulate enough cash to cover at least one to three months' living expenses — Do so before mid-1999. If we should have a one-day to one-month banking holiday in 1999 or 2000, cash will be king. There are likely to be some super-pessimists, who, fearing a bank run, pull all of their funds out of the banks by mid-1999. I would not counsel such a course of action, but bank runs may occur in certain areas around the world. If you do pull a few months' living expenses out of your bank, be careful not to violate any federal bank secrecy (money laundering/ structuring) laws.

6) Consider acquiring up to 35 percent of an investment portfolio in gold and silver coins — Two-thirds in semi-numismatic gold coins and one-third in silver coins

(U.S. junk silver coins and silver dollars). The supply of U.S. double eagles is now tighter than it has been in 25 years. They have become very difficult to obtain! This is true of certain bullion coins as well. Knowledgeable investors who understand the approaching global financial disaster (not even considering the Y2K crisis) have been quietly buying up available coins. Supplies are very short.

Gold coins should be acquired in retirement funds (IRAs, Keoghs, SEPs and other pension funds) if you are not expressly precluded from doing so. For information or assistance in acquiring gold or silver coins or to receive a free investment strategy package (or for doing IRA or other pension fund rollovers into gold or silver), call International Collectors Associates at 1-800-525-9556.

7) Determine if companies and institutions with which you do business are Y2K-compliant — Dr. Gary North has suggested the following letter to send to such businesses:

> I'm concerned about something I have been reading about in the press. It's a real problem: the disruption of computers beginning on January 1, 2000. This is sometimes called the Millennium Bug: "2000" is entered as "00." Mainframe computers recognize this as 1900 instead of 2000.
>
> What I need to know is this: Has your organization had all of its mainframe computer code repaired? Second, have all of your computer systems (including the programs on PC desktop computers) been certified year 2000 compliant?
>
> If your organization is not yet compliant, on what date did you begin the repair? How many

programmers are now working on the project? Finally, how many lines of code are in your system?

I have placed my confidence in your organization. I want written assurance that I will not suffer financially from my continued reliance on your services as a result of your organization's failure to make the January 1, 2000 deadline, or the failure to meet this deadline by organizations with which your computer shares data or on which your organization relies. I am depending on you. Please let me know as soon as possible. Time is of the essence.

If your bank, broker, insurance company, or other supplier isn't aware of the problem, doesn't have a compliance plan, or is in denial regarding the problem, you might want to switch to another entity that is compliant or about to become compliant.

8) If you have a small business, make sure your computers and software are Y2K compliant — Not all PCs are compliant. My investment firm is replacing 16 non-compliant personal computers as part of our Y2K compliance program. Do not procrastinate. Begin your Y2K repair now! Give it top priority in your business. It will cost you money, but it may save your business. Also make sure your suppliers are Y2K compliant or rapidly becoming so. Macintosh computers and their operating systems are okay, but check your applications and data files.

9) Keep good personal paper records of all your financial dealings — File paper copies of records from your bank, S&L, insurance company, pension fund, credit union, utilities, phone company, credit card companies, Social Security, Medicare, the IRS, state and local tax

authorities, etc. If their computers go haywire, you need to have backup records to prove the status of your accounts.

Conclusion

With the Y2K crisis, the Asian financial meltdown, and other potentially disruptive events looming on the horizon, the need to plan ahead and stockpile useful items becomes more urgent. Even people who have traditionally been unconcerned about preparedness have become more conscious of being ready for hard times in recent months, as Y2K-related stories have recently appeared everywhere from national publications to obscure local weeklies.

Since there is a limited amount of time before Y2K-related disruptions may begin to cripple normal activity, it would be easy to take a fatalistic attitude that nothing can be done or that it is useless or unnecessary to take precautionary actions.

Such an attitude is wrong at best, and could be very harmful to you and your family over the next few years. While almost everyone has financial limitations, there is much that can be done by anyone regardless of your circumstances to put yourself in a better position to withstand Y2K-related chaos. Even the person of modest means can fare better than the vast majority, provided that prudent action is taken immediately.

Even though Y2K has become a hot topic in recent months, public awareness of the problem is like the Mississippi River — a mile wide and an inch deep. The average American who has read an article or two on Y2K has concluded that there is a potential computer breakdown way "out there" in the distant future. Many hope that Bill

Gates or some other techno-genius will gallop John Wayne-style to the rescue with a solution just in time.

In the best-case scenario, multitudes of date-related mainframe problems will commence on January 1, 2000. In reality, many such glitches have already begun, and they will become very apparent and far more numerous in coming months. Many state and local governments, as well as privately owned companies, operate on fiscal years that have little to do with a January through December calendar. For many annual budgets, fiscal year 2000 will begin as early as June 1, 1999. Banks and other creditors calculate principal and interest payments well into the future.

As year 2000 payments begin to become an issue, the buried problems in financial software and bank mainframes will suddenly emerge and wreak havoc. While even establishment insiders are admitting that Y2K is a very thorny problem, no one can say for sure just how serious or long-lasting it will be. There is no historical precedent for making comparisons.

However, there is an opportunity to minimize some of the potential suffering beforehand. Wide public reaction to Y2K will come in the future, but that is still months away. For at least the next several months, you will have a head start on getting ready for what could be some very challenging times.

The wise person who plans ahead and stockpiles supplies will be able to ride out the crisis with much less anguish and inconvenience. Items that are widely available and common today could become all but unobtainable (even at much higher prices) as we near January 1, 2000.

You may not be able to acquire everything described in this chapter. You may not have the time, the finances, the storage space, or perhaps even the motivation to do it all. This is simply a checklist of things to consider in your Y2K thinking, strategizing, and preparedness planning. Most of the suggestions in this chapter can be implemented to some degree regardless of your financial means, age, or physical location. The suggested items to stockpile are available now, but many will probably not be available when the final panic begins. It will be much easier to acquire some of these items in a more rural, country, or small-town environment (well, water storage, wood stove, generator, personal protection).

If you are serious about Y2K preparations, it is essential that you sit down with your family and do your planning now. Prioritize your plan; set aside a budget for acquiring or accomplishing the top priorities; set up a schedule; and try to have most of the important tasks or acquisitions made as soon as possible.

Obstacles to Y2K Preparation

There will be a number of obstacles in becoming prepared for Y2K — most of them will be mental and emotional: 1) apathy, complacency, the "it can't really happen"/denial attitude; 2) a spouse or family member who is in denial or doesn't understand, and is, therefore, opposed to making preparations (family unity will be very important); 3) ridicule from friends, family or co-workers (the solution to this is to not tell them what you are doing); 4) discouragement over the size of the task and the little time remaining. You probably can't do it all, but you can do a lot if you start right now and make it a major priority in your life.

Every time you shop, double or triple up on the items you regularly use, and in a year, you will have most of the substantial supplies you need.

Remember, preparedness is a state of mind. It is a never-ending process. Many people will feel over-whelmed and frustrated by the size of the task and by the thought of preparing for something they hope will never happen. The more heightened your awareness of the problem, the more motivated you will be to prepare.

I strongly encourage readers to develop a sense of urgency and to prepare physically, mentally, emotionally, socially, and most important of all — spiritually. The God of the Bible does not want us to be fearful or to panic. As 2 Timothy 1:7 says, "For God has not given us a spirit of fear, but of power, and love and sound mind."

In my opinion and in the light of the Bible, the Lord wants us to understand the times we live in; to be prepared for the times; to seek his wisdom, guidance, and direction on how to navigate through the troubled waters that lie ahead; to trust Him for our ultimate protection; and to serve Him as the foundations crumble. The opportunities to help others who are not prepared and to share the love of Christ with those who have lost those things upon which they have based their security are going to be very challenging indeed. The most exciting, and perhaps most spiritually productive, times of our lives lie immediately ahead!

An Ongoing Source of Information:
The McAlvany Intelligence Advisor

The McAlvany Intelligence Advisor (*MIA*) is a monthly monetary, economic, political, geopolitical newsletter written from a biblical/traditionalist perspective. *MIA* provides in-depth analysis of domestic and global developments such as the Asian financial crisis; the coming financial collapse and upheaval in America; the present political scandals in Washington; the global plunge toward a cash-less society and world government; the emerging new axis — China/Russia/radical Islam; China's preparation for war against the West within the next decade; the coming war in the Middle East; alternative medicine; financial preparations for the coming depression; attaining greater self-sufficiency; and dozens of other topics to better help readers to understand the times and prepare confidently for the future.

A subscription costs $115 for one year (that's only 31.5 cents per day), or $185 for two years (only 25.3 cents per day). In order to subscribe or to receive two free sample issues of *MIA*, call 800-525-9556. Hosea 4:6 says, "My people are destroyed from lack of knowledge." *The McAlvany Intelligence Advisor* can give you ongoing knowledge, insights, and perspectives that you will need to survive and prosper as we move into the new millennium.

Reading Materials and Other Resources

It has been said that "action without knowledge leads to confusion and chaos." There is a lot of excellent reading material on the millennium Y2K crisis that can help those interested in the topic.

Books and Reports

1) *The Millennium Meltdown: The Year 2000 Computer Crisis* by Grant Jeffrey (Toronto: Frontier Research Publications, 1998).

   1) *Time Bomb 2000: What the Year 2000 Computer Crisis*

Means to You by Edward and Jennifer Yourdon (Prentice Hall PTR, 1998).

3) *The Year 2000 Software Problem: Quantifying the Cost and Assessing the Consequences* by Capers Jones (New York: ACM Press, 1997).

4) *The Coming Dark Age* by Roberto Vacca, (Doubleday, 1973). This book, which describes life in the cities when the infrastructure support systems break down, is probably out of print, but it can be obtained at a library.

5) *How to Survive and Prosper After the Year 2000 Computer Crash* by David Price (Grapevine Publications, P.O. Box 45047, Boise, Idaho 83711; 208-345-3669; $10). An excellent overview of the Y2K problem and strategy for survival, which was very helpful in the writing of this book.

6) *Does the "Year 2000 Problem" Present Dangers for Your Family?* by Steve Gregg (November 1997). A preparation manual written from a biblical perspective. (Write to: Home Aid Letters Magazine, P.O. Box 1274, McMinnville, Oregon 97128; $5.00).

7) *Strategic Relocation North American Guide to Safe Places*— Joel Skousen, 290 West 580 South, Orem, Utah 45058; 801-224-4746; $45. An excellent guide on relocation for those inclined to do so. Skousen also has other excellent books on survival/self-sufficiency architecture.

Significant Y2K Magazine Articles

1) "The Day the World Shut Down," *Newsweek* (June 2, 1997).

2) "Millennium Bug Muddle — Why Great Technologies Cause Great Mistakes," *The Economist* (October 4, 1997).

3) How The Year 2000 Bug Will Hurt the Economy (It's Worse Than You Think)," *Business Week* (March 2, 1998).

Recommended Newsletters

1) *McAlvany Intelligence Advisor* (Donald S. McAlvany; PO Box 84904, Phoenix, Az 85071; 800-528—0559; $115/year).

2) *Remnant Review* (Dr. Gary North; 1217 St. Paul Street, Baltimore, MD 21202; 410-234-0691; $129/year). Gary North has written more on the coming Millennium Bug crisis than any other newsletter writer over the past 24 months.

3) *Year 2000 Journal* (Robert Thomas; P.O. Box 550547, Dallas, TX 75355-0547; 214-340-2147; web site: www.y2kjournal.com; $96 per year).

4) *Personal Update* (Chuck Missler, Koinonia House, P.O. Box D, Coeur d'Alene, ID 83816-0347; 208-773-6310; http://www.khouse.org.). A series of radio tapes on Y2K featuring Chuck Missler, John Loeffler, and Don McAlvany are also available through Koinonia House.

Internet Sites That Contain Relevant Y2K Information

1) www.mcalvany.com: The ICA Y2K Preparedness Center. Financial Strategies & Personal Preparation and Don McAlvany's Audio Intelligence Report

2) www.garynorth.com: Gary North's Y2K Links and Forums. An excellent source of Y2K information from many sources.

3) www.y2kchaos.com A comprehensive site with information pertaining to all aspects of Y2K and Y2K preparedness.

4) www.yourdon.com: Edward Yourdon's site. Yourdon has been quoted extensively in this book.

5) www.yardeni.com: Dr. Edward Yardeni's site.

6) www.y2ktimebomb.com: Jim Lord's site sponsored by Westergaard Year 2000.

7) www.year2000.com: Year 2000 Information Center. This site is maintained by Peter de Jager (a Canadian author).

8) www.millennia-bcs.com/hlthsmry.htm: This is a good Y2K site sponsored by the Casandra Project and is maintained by Paloma O'Riley.

9) www.y2kwomen.com: What every woman needs to know in dealing with Y2K.

10) www.2000digest.com/ydkbug.html: Good Y2K information and links.

Video Tapes

1) *Countdown to the Year 2000*: Video Tapes by Don McAlvany on the Millennium Bug Crisis. Six hours of video tapes from the Southern California Conference.

Tape 1:The Rogue Wave: The Financial, Political, and Social Decline of America

Tape 2: Storm Warning: The Asian/global Financial Meltdown is Headed For America

Tape 3: The Millennium Bug: Global Cyber-meltdown in the Year 2000

Tape 4: Getting Out of Harm's Way: Preparing for the Coming Financial Upheaval in America

These tapes can be used to bring family, friends, pastors, church members, and others up to speed on the Y2K crisis, the coming financial upheaval, and what people need to do to prepare. They are especially useful for group discussions.

2) *The Millennium Bug and the Year 2000* (Ken Klein Ministries, Box 40922, Eugene, OR 97404; 800-888-1363 $24.90).

3) *The Millennium Meltdown*. Grant R. Jeffrey, Frontier Research Publications Inc. 800-883-1812.

Other Resources

1) Food Reserves and Precious Metals Source: International Collectors Associates (800-525-9556).

2) Essential Oils Source: Essential Oils Healthline PO Box 17137, Fountain Hills, AZ,85269; 602-430-3300).

17

A Biblical Perspective on the Y2K Crisis

Has America Forgotten God?

Alexander Solzhenitsyn, the great Russian dissident, was once asked on BBC television why the Russian people lost their freedom to the Communists. His instant reply was, "We forgot God." Is it possible that sometime in the not too distant future America will implode socially, culturally, politically, and financially and that a post-mortem on a fallen America will show that we too "forgot God"?

Why would a country "forget God"? Because of pain, suffering, poverty, depression, or war? Probably not! Pain and suffering build character and send individuals and nations back to the basics, and often, back to God. Conversely, great wealth, affluence, and prosperity, combined with sensuality, materialism, great leisure, and boredom are destructive to character and often lead individuals and nations away from God.

In the past half century America has enjoyed the greatest prosperity and affluence of any country in the history of the world. As a nation we are very proud of our accomplishments, our power, our wealth, and affluence, and our high technology. We are the only superpower in the world. But what has happened to our national character, our morality, our virtue, our sense of right versus wrong? During the recent decades of affluence, they have suffered immeasurably!

Today, in fact, we lead the world in promiscuity; in homosexuality; in incest; in sexual abuse of children; in rape; in murder and other violent crimes; in drug use and alcoholism; in pornography; in divorce and single-parent families; in suicide; in abortion; in children murdering other children; in lawsuits; and in unadulterated greed, as exemplified by the 1990s speculative binge on Wall Street, the gambling craze, etc. At what cost are we pursuing the goals of wealth and material gain?

Is America today truly strong? Or are we ready for a great fall — like ancient Babylon, Persia, Greece, Israel, Rome, Russia in 1917, Germany in the 1930s, or South Africa in 1994? All of these nations were also number one in their region or in the world until they suddenly fell. They were also very proud and arrogant.

In America today we have a president who epitomizes many of the ills of our nation and yet 60–70 percent of the American people are so blinded by their present wealth, affluence, and prosperity through the rising stock market that they no longer can see the evil that Bill Clinton represents, object to it, or in any way oppose it. America today is in many ways a reflection of the behavior and character of Clinton.

The same can be said of the U.S. Congress — Republicans and Democrats. Our wealth, affluence, and prosperity have blinded and corrupted us. Alexis de Toqueville once said, "America is great because America is good. If America ever ceases to be good, she will cease to be great." Rereading that list of our unrighteous deeds above, one can say with certainty that America in the late 1990s has ceased to be good. We are a sick nation — and yet in our great pride and arrogance, we still see ourselves as number one. The Bible says, "Pride comes before a fall."

History reveals that great nations rise, they become prosperous, they become corrupted, and they fall. Is America any different? If we continue on our present course, this nation will fall — whether from a financial meltdown; Y2K; Chinese, Russian or Islamic nuclear missiles; or to an internal dictator — the next Hitler, Lenin, Stalin, or Mao Tse Tung.

So what is the answer for America? In my opinion, only a national revival — genuine repentance and turning back to God — will save America. The ancient city of Nineveh had a profound revival around 725 BC. The Old Testament book of Jonah describes how the Lord was about to destroy the evil and corrupt nation of Assyria. God sent a reluctant Jonah to Nineveh, the capital of Assyria, to warn the people of the Lord's judgment and their coming destruction. The people repented of their wickedness and turned to the Lord, so the Lord spared Nineveh from its destruction for a number of years.

The same thing could happen in America. A great revival could bring us back from the brink of collapse. Will it happen? Only the Lord knows, but it is something worth praying for. Without it, I believe America will be judged by God. As 2 Chronicles 7:14 says, "If my people, who are called by my name will humble themselves and pray and seek my face and turn from their wicked ways, then will I hear from heaven and will forgive their sin and will heal their land."

Sadly, I believe that most Americans will not remember God or turn back to him until they have lost their prosperity and perhaps their freedom, both of which could happen over the next few years.

Nevertheless, God will still look after His faithful remnant, who remember Him, obey Him, and follow Him. As Isaiah 49:29–31 says, "He will give strength to the weary, and increase the power of the weak . . . but those who hope in the Lord will renew their strength. They will soar on wings like eagles; they will run and not grow weary, they will walk and not faint." Isaiah 41:10 says, "So do not fear, for I am with you. Do not be dismayed for I am your God. I will strengthen you and help you. I will uphold you with my righteous right hand."

God's Command to a Nation That Wishes to Prosper

The book of Deuteronomy records God's admonitions to the people of Israel. He tells Israel what will happen if they follow His decrees and what will happen if they ignore or forget them. America would be wise to follow these same principles in our day:

> Hear now, O Israel, the decrees and laws I am about to teach you. Follow them so that you may live . . . Do not add to what I command you, and do not subtract from it, but keep the commands of the Lord your God that I give you.
>
> Deuteronomy 4:1–2

And what other nation is so great as to have such righteous decrees and laws as this body of laws I am setting before you today. Only be careful, and watch yourselves closely so that you do not forget the things your eyes have seen or let them slip from your hearts as long as you live. Teach them to your children, and their children after them.

Deuteronomy 4:8–9

Therefore, watch yourselves very carefully, so that you do not become corrupt . . ." vs. 24: "For the Lord your God is a consuming fire, a jealous God. After you have had children and grandchildren and have lived in the land a long time — if you then become corrupt and make any kind of idol, doing evil in the eyes of the Lord your God and provoking him to anger, I call heaven and earth as witnesses against you this day that you will quickly perish from the land that you are crossing the Jordan to possess. You will not live there long but will certainly be destroyed.

Deuteronomy 4:15b–16a

But if from there you seek the Lord your God, you will find him if you look for him with all your heart and with all your soul. When you are in distress and all these things have happened to you, then in later days, you will return to the Lord your God and obey him. For the Lord your God is a merciful God; he will not abandon or destroy you or forget the covenant with your forefathers, which he confirmed to them by oath. . . . Keep his decrees and commands, which I am giving you today, so that it may go well with you and your children after you and that you may live long in the land the Lord your God gives you for all time.

Deuteronomy 4:29–31

So be careful to do what the Lord your God has commanded you; do not turn aside to the right or to the left. Walk in all the way that the Lord your God has commanded you, so that you may live and prosper and prolong your days in the land that you will possess.

Deuteronomy 5:32–33

When you have eaten and are satisfied, praise the Lord your God for the good land he has given you. Be careful that you do not forget the Lord your God, failing to observe his commands, his laws, and his decrees that I am giving you this day. Otherwise, when you eat and are satisfied, when you build fine houses and settle down, and when your herd and flocks grow large and your silver and gold increase and all you have is multiplied, then your heart will become proud and you will forget the Lord your God.

You now say to yourself 'my power and the strength of my herds have produced this wealth for me. But remember the Lord your God, for it is he who gives you the ability to produce wealth. . . . If you ever forget the Lord your God and follow other gods and worship and bow down to them, I testify against you today that you will surely be destroyed. Like the nations the Lord destroyed before you, so you will be destroyed for not obeying the Lord your God.

Deuteronomy 8:10-14a, 17, 19–20

See, I am setting before you a blessing and a curse — the blessing if you obey the commands of the Lord your God that I am giving you today; the curse if you disobey the commands of the Lord your God and turn away from the way that I command you today by following other gods.

Deuteronomy 11:26

Much of the story of the Old Testament is about Israel turning its back on God, getting in trouble, turning back to God, and then turning away from Him again, repeating the cycle. The Old Testament books of Isaiah, Jeremiah, and others describe God's judgment of His people when they turned away from Him and disobeyed his commands.

America is at a spiritual crossroads. Either we turn, as a nation, back to God, remember His commands and follow them, or the judgments that fell on Israel (i.e., wicked leaders, the enslavement of the people, conquest by foreign nations) will befall America and the West.

Are We, as a Nation, Choosing Life or Death?

In the book of Deuteronomy, the choice of a path of spiritual life or a path of death is set before the nation of Israel:

See, I set before you today life and prosperity, death and destruction. For I command you today to love the Lord your God, to walk in his ways, and to keep his commands, decrees, and laws; then you will live and increase, and the Lord your God will bless you in the land you are entering to possess.

But if your heart turns away and you are not obedient, and if you are drawn away to bow down to other Gods and worship them, I declare to you this day that you will certainly be destroyed . . . I have set before you life and death, blessings and curses. Now choose life, that you and your children might live, and that you might love the Lord your God, listen to his voice, and hold fast to him.

Deuteronomy 32:15–19

At this point in our history, it appears as if America (in its 1992 and 1996 elections) is choosing the path of spiritual death. Just as the people of Germany chose to support a man and a movement in the 1930s that stood for death, destruction, immorality, and pagan gods, so the American people may have made a similar choice.

In Deuteronomy 28, the Lord laid out the blessings He provides to a nation that obeys and follows Him and His ways and the curses that follow a nation that disobeys Him and goes its own way. Forget, for a moment, the politics or the charisma of the two major candidates in the recent presidential race and just consider morality, ethics, integrity, and a belief in traditional values.

The American people in 1992 and 1996 chose a president who was a draft dodger, a drug user, an adulterer, an advocate of the killing of unborn babies, and a defender of the homosexual agenda. He also has a record of opposing traditional biblical values.

The other choice was a military veteran of World War II; who never used drugs; was faithful to his wife; stated that he was against abortion; has never defended, endorsed, or promoted the homosexual lifestyle; and has at least verbally defended the traditional, Biblical values that are under massive attack in America today.

The American people have chosen spiritual death and rejected life.

A nation that kills more than one million unborn babies per year; that practices widespread immorality, promiscuity; that endorses homosexuality; that leads the world in production of pornography, the use of drugs, in violent crime, in divorce, in teenage pregnancies and suicide — in short, a nation that has forgotten and disobeyed God, is certainly ripe for God's judgment.

That judgment could take several forms: economic instability and depression; social decline and collapse; disease and plague; military disasters; weather disturbances and natural catastrophes; the loss of our children to drugs, rebellion, and immorality; occupation by foreigners (UN or other foreign troops); rulership by cruel and wicked leaders (God gives a nation the leaders it deserves); persecution of good and godly people; and the loss of freedom.

The potential for all of these judgments seems to be growing dramatically, especially as the Y2K disaster approaches. Nevertheless, to those individuals who follow the God of the Bible, who obey His principles and precepts, who remain faithful to Him while the great majority are turning away, God promises His blessings, protection, and strength. Just as God provided a place of refuge for Noah and his family in that day of great trouble, so He can do the same for us today.

For those who are discouraged by recent developments, the Bible has some strong words of encouragement. Deuteronomy 33:27 says, "The eternal God is your refuge, and underneath are his everlasting arms. He will drive out your enemy before you." In 2 Samuel 22:2–3, David wrote, "The Lord is my rock, my fortress and my deliverer; my God is my rock, in whom I take refuge . . . He is my stronghold, my refuge, and my savior. He is a shield for all who take refuge in Him."

Troubled times may lie ahead for America. This book has discussed many means to self-sufficiency — finances, food, health and medicine, country living — but our ultimate shelter and refuge in a time of storm lie in the hands of the living God.

The message of the Bible is that in times of trouble, when the foundations are crumbling, the God of the Bible is an ever-present help and refuge — a hiding place for His people.

Chasing After the Wind

America, like the ancient Roman Empire, is a great nation in decline. And yet America (the world's leading super-power) is the richest, most affluent, most prosperous country not only in the world today, but in world history. We Americans are the most entertained, most pleasure-seeking, most materialistic, most fun-oriented people in world history. We have more leisure time, more toys, and more entertainment distractions than any other nation on earth. But has all of this material abundance, affluence, entertainment, and sensual distraction made the American people a happy people?

There is an interesting parallel in the Bible with America today, found in the life of the most powerful, richest, affluent, king in Israel's history — King Solomon.

The book of Ecclesiastes, written by Solomon in his latter years, describes in detail how this powerful king sought happiness and satisfaction in wealth, power, materialism, women, entertainment, and hard work. In the ancient world his kingdom was unsurpassed in wealth, splendor, and grandeur.

Solomon, like people in America in its earlier years, began his life walking very closely to the God of the Bible. He was blessed with a strong character passed down to him from his father, King David, and endowed by the Lord with great wisdom. It was in his earlier years as king that he wrote the book of Proverbs. However, as his life of wealth and affluence progressed, he turned away from God, and his character deteriorated. The book of Ecclesiastes describes the cumulative effect of Solomon's spiritual decline and idolatry. He began to worship the false gods worshipped by his pagan wives and engaged in a life of self-indulgence. However, by the end of his life he had become disillusioned with materialism and pleasure as a way to happiness.

Ecclesiastes records Solomon's cynical reflections about the futility and emptiness of seeking happiness in life's pleasures, apart from God and his Scriptures. "Meaningless! Meaningless! Everything is meaningless and chasing after the wind," Solomon repeatedly said. The word "meaningless" is actually repeated 37 times in this book. He makes a strong case of the futility of basing ones values in life on earthly possessions and personal ambition, and concludes that it is far more important to commit oneself to his (or her) Creator (Eccl. 12:1) and to resolve to fear God and keep His commandments (Eccl. 12:13–14) as the only path to genuine meaning in life.

Solomon's experiences and conclusions describe many Americans today, who, though they may have great abundance, affluence, material well-being and pleasure are nevertheless empty and find life meaningless — like "chasing the wind."

If this spiritual emptiness characterizes the majority of Americans today, could this explain America's incredible moral, social, spiritual, political decline as a nation? Is the stampede for wealth, materialism, and sensuality in America today simply the meaningless chasing after the wind that Solomon described in Ecclesiastes?

Solomon's conclusion that man should "fear God and keep his commandments," and the New Testament admonition that a personal relationship with the God of the Bible, through His Son, Jesus Christ, is the only real road to happiness, contentment, peace, and eternal life with God, is the only substantive answer for tens of millions of frustrated, empty Americans who are spending their lives "chasing the wind."

Losing the Good Life:
Finding Freedom in an Unfree World

The next two to three years could bring convulsive changes to America and most of the world — changes that not one in a hundred, or perhaps one in a thousand, people see coming, or are prepared for. As I Thessalonians 5:3 says, "While people are saying, 'Peace and safety,' destruction will come on them suddenly, as labor pains on a pregnant woman, and they will not escape."

Many Americans will lose their "good life" — their wealth, possessions, economic security, and perhaps even their freedom. However, the Lord promises his followers that "my God will meet all your needs according to his glorious riches in Christ Jesus" in Philippians 4:19.

Jesus had some strong words of encouragement in Matthew 6:25–34 for those who are worried about their future:

> Therefore I tell you, do not worry about your life, what you will eat or drink; or about your body, what you will wear. Is not life more important than food, and the body more important than clothes? Look at the birds of the air; they do not sow or reap or store away in barns, and yet your heavenly Father feeds them. Are you not much more valuable than they? Who of you by worrying can add a single hour to his life?

> And why do you worry about clothes? See how the lilies of the field grow. They do not labor or spin. Yet I tell you that not even Solomon in all his splendor was dressed like one of these. If that is how God clothes the grass of the field, which is here today and tomorrow is thrown into the fire, will he not much more clothe you, O you of little faith? So do not worry, saying, 'What shall we eat?' or 'What shall we drink?' or 'What shall we wear?' For the pagans run after all these things, and your heavenly Father knows that you need them. But seek first His kingdom and His righteousness, and all these things will be given to you as well. Therefore do not worry about tomorrow. . . .

Is There a Time to Flee?

The Bible is replete with examples of God's people fleeing from, or hiding from, disaster. David fled from King Saul; Lot fled from Sodom; Elijah fled from Rahab and Jezebel; Moses escaped from Pharaoh; and Jesus avoided his persecutors "until his hour came" at the Garden of Gethsemane [Luke 4:28–30, John 8:59, 10:39, 12:36]. Paul also did a lot of escaping, although he was in no sense averse to dying and going to be with the Lord (Phil. 1:21–23). He, like many other believers, simply exercised reasonable caution so as not to prematurely shorten his life and ministry.

In the history of Christianity, Christians have frequently fled from dangerous places to safer ones. Jewish believers escaped from Jerusalem before the holocaust of AD 70 when Roman Emperor Titus killed over one million Jews in that city. In 1685, 400,000 Huguenots fled France to escape persecution. Moravians fled en masse from their native Moravia to Zinzendorf's estate in Germany, and Armenian believers escaped to America before the Turkish massacre of those who remained behind.

Thousands of believers have fled the persecution in the former Soviet Union, Red China, and Cuba, even though other believers remained in those countries and functioned secretly in the underground church. Many who remained by choice, necessity, or by the clear will of the Lord were imprisoned and/or martyred for their faith.

In Luke 21, Jesus was asked by His disciples on the Mount of Olives what would be the signs of His return and the end of the age. He responded by describing a period of great deception, persecution, betrayal, and suffering. In Luke 21:20–21, He also warned of foreign armies coming against Jerusalem and indicated that believers should hastily escape the danger: "When you see Jerusalem being surrounded by armies, you will know that its destruction is near. Then let those who are in Judea flee to the mountains, let those in the city get out, and let those in the country not enter the city."

In a future period of chaos and upheaval in America (perhaps Y2K-related), some people who understand the times will move out of the cities and into a small town, or the country. This author, his family, and company did so almost seven years ago. Others will choose to remain in the cities because the Lord directs them to do so. However, many who remain in the cities will make no preparations because of apathy, complacency, laziness, or denial. These people may fare very poorly over the next few years.

In my view, the place to be, as well as your level of preparedness, should be based on the Lord's guidance and direction in your life. As Isaiah 58:11 says, "The Lord will guide you always; he will satisfy your needs in a sun-scorched land and will strengthen your frame." Psalm 37:23 says, "The steps of a good man are ordered by the Lord . . ." Psalm 107:30 says, ". . . and He guided them to their desired haven." If a person seeks the Lord on the matters discussed in this book, I believe that the Lord will give him or her wisdom, guidance, discernment, and insight to decide what to do or where to go.

The bottom line is, if there is a time to flee, flee into the arms of the Lord, and everything else will fall into place.

Warnings

Throughout the history of the world, God has always made known to His people impending times of trouble, and He has given them time to prepare (or escape):

• He warned Noah and his family of the coming flood and directed them how to prepare to survive it.

• God warned Lot and his family of the coming destruction of Sodom and Gomorrah and told them to flee.

• The Lord warned Pharaoh, through Joseph, of the coming famine and used Joseph to prepare stores of food during the seven years of plenty, which saved Egypt and Joseph's family when the famine came.

• God warned the Israelites, who lived under Egyptian slavery that the "angel of death" would kill all the first-born of every family and that they must protect themselves and their families by placing the blood of a lamb over the doorposts, so that the angel would "passover" them.

• He warned the people of Israel through his prophet Isaiah of the coming conquest of the Northern Kingdom by Assyria. This happened in 712 BC.

• The Lord warned the people of Judah (the Southern Kingdom) through his prophet Jeremiah, of their coming conquest by Babylon. This happened in 586 BC.

• Jonah was sent to Ninevah, the capital city of Assyria, to warn this pagan people of God's coming destruction. When they repented, God postponed the judgment for a number of years.

• Jesus warned the people of Jerusalem of their coming destruction by Rome: "As he (Jesus) approached Jerusalem and saw the city, he wept over it and said 'If you, even you, had only known on this day what would bring you peace — but now it is hidden from your eyes. The days will come upon you when your enemies will build an embankment against you and encircle you and hem you in on every side. They will dash you to the ground, you and the children within your walls. They will not leave one stone on another, because you did not recognize the time of God's coming to you" (Luke 19:41–44).

When Jerusalem fell to the Romans, almost 40 years later in 70 AD, most of Jesus' followers had already fled the city and scattered. Over one million Jews were killed in Jerusalem at that time by the Romans under Titus.

In Europe, during the 1930s, many Christians and Jews were given discernment by the Lord. They recognized the dark clouds of death and destruction that were rolling across Europe and were able to get out before the Nazi boot slammed down on the continent. There were warnings that many of God's people acted upon, thereby escaping with their family out of harm's way.

The history of the Christian church — a period of almost 2000 years — has been checkered with numerous persecutions. The Lord has given advanced warnings of the coming persecutions to His followers, so that they might flee, prepare for the trials — spiritually or physically, or go underground. In almost every one of those situations, it was primarily the God-fearing remnant who had the discernment to understand the times, to see the destruction and suffering that was coming, and to prepare (physically and spiritually).

One common denominator in almost all of those times of trouble down through the ages, is that the great majority of people could not see the upheaval coming. They refused to believe it. They were in denial. They were enjoying the good life (eating, drinking and partying) right up until the disaster overtook them. And, nothing was going to make them believe otherwise. Today, the Y2K crisis and global financial meltdown approaching like a freight train out of control, is no different.

As Jesus said regarding the people of Noah's day in Matthew 24:38–39, "For in the days before the flood, people were eating and drinking, marrying and giving in marriage up to the day Noah entered the Ark; and they knew nothing about what would happen until the flood came and took them all away."

The same is happening in America today, but a growing number of people in the remnant have awakened to the political and financial upheaval that Y2K is likely to bring to America in a matter of months. They are taking steps to get out of harm's way, to protect their families, and to prepare for a time of great trouble.

The times that lie ahead will try the souls of men. They will be both challenging and exciting. They will offer great opportunities for those who have heeded the warnings to help those who have not prepared materially, and to share the saving truth about Jesus Christ — the ultimate security in an insecure world.

Readers of this book are encouraged to seek the Lord for wisdom, guidance, and direction on how they should live, prepare and serve the Lord in the next few years. The God of the Bible will warn His followers and will take care of His people!

ORDER FORM

Quantity	Code	Description	Price	Total
		Softback Books		
	BK-3	Messiah – War in the Middle East & The Road to Armageddon	$12.99	
	BK-4	Apocalypse – The Coming Judgment of the Nations	$12.99	
	BK-5	Prince of Darkness – Antichrist and the New World Order	$13.99	
	BK-6	Final Warning – Economic Collapse and Coming World Government	$13.99	
	BK-7	Heaven – The Mystery of Angels	$12.99	
	BK-8	The Signature of God – Astonishing Biblical Discoveries	$13.99	
	BK-9	Yeshua – The Name of Jesus Revealed in the O.T. (Rambsel)	$11.99	
	BK-10	Armageddon – Appointment With Destiny	$12.99	
	BK-11	His Name is Jesus – The Mysterious Yeshua Codes (Rambsel)	$12.99	
	BK-12	The Handwriting of God – Sacred Mysteries of the Bible	$13.99	
	BK-13	The Millennium Meltdown – Year 2000 Computer Crisis	$13.99	
	BK-14	The New World Religion (Kah)	$12.99	
	BK-15	The Y2K Tidal Wave (McAlvany)		
		ANY THREE BOOKS OR MORE **EACH**	**$11.00**	
		Videos		
	V-5	The Rebirth of Israel and The Messiah	$19.99	
	V-7	The Rapture and Heaven's Glory	$19.99	
	V-8	The Coming Millennial Kingdom	$19.99	
	V-9	The Search for The Messiah	$19.99	
	V-12	Financial Strategies and Assault on Our Freedom	$19.99	
	V-13	Archeological Discoveries: Exploring Beneath the Temple Mount	$19.99	
	V-14	Prince of Darkness and The Final Inquisition	$19.99	
	V-15	Agenda of The New World Order and The Tribulation	$19.99	
	V-16	Rush to Armageddon	$19.99	
	V-19	The Millennium Meltdown	$19.99	
		ANY TWO VIDEOS OR MORE **EACH**	**$17.00**	
		Hardcover Books		
	HC-H	Heaven – The Mystery of Angels	$19.99	
		Executive Edition *(pocket-sized witnessing pack)*		
	EE-1	The Signature of God (78 pages, 3 booklets per pack)	$9.99	
		Total this page (to be carried forward)		

continued overleaf

ORDER FORM

Quantity	Code	Description	Price	Total
			Total from previous page	
		Double-length Videos		
	V-17	The Signature of God – Astonishing Biblical Discoveries	$34.99	
	V-18	Mysterious Bible Codes	$29.99	
	VP-1	Final Warning, Big Brother Government	$29.99	
		Audio Cassettes		
	AB-14	The Signature of God (2 tapes)	$15.99	
	AB-15	Mysterious Bible Codes (2 tapes)	$15.99	
	AB-16	The Millennium Meltdown (2 tapes)	$15.99	
	AP-01	Super Money Management for Christians (6 tapes)	$39.99	
	PIB	**Product Brochure**	No charge	
		Oklahoma residents add 7.5% sales tax		
		Canadian residents add 7% G.S.T.		
		One low shipping and handling fee (per order) for U.S. and Canada	$4.95	$4.95

*Additional shipping charges will apply to orders
outside North America*

Grand Total

U.S. orders: mail along with your check or money order to mail-order house:
Frontier Research Publications • P.O. Box 470470 • Tulsa, OK 74147-0470

U.S. credit card orders: call 1-800-883-1812

Canadian orders: remit payment to head office:
Frontier Research Publications • P.O. Box 129, Station "U" • Toronto, Ontario M8Z 5M4

Canadian VISA/MasterCard orders: call 1-800-853-1423

Prices effective January 1, 1999

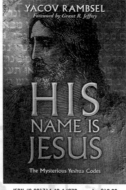
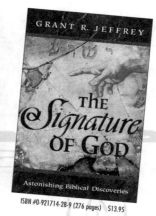

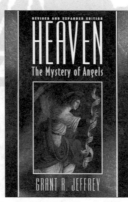